CAMBRIDGE LIBRARY COLLECTION

Books of enduring scholarly value

Perspectives from the Royal Asiatic Society

A long-standing European fascination with Asia, from the Middle East to
China and Japan, came more sharply into focus during the early modern
period, as voyages of exploration gave rise to commercial enterprises such
as the East India companies, and their attendant colonial activities. This
series is a collaborative venture between the Cambridge Library Collection
and the Royal Asiatic Society of Great Britain and Ireland, founded in 1823.
The series reissues works from the Royal Asiatic Society's extensive library
of rare books and sponsored publications that shed light on eighteenth- and
nineteenth-century European responses to the cultures of the Middle East and
Asia. The selection covers Asian languages, literature, religions, philosophy,
historiography, law, mathematics and science, as studied and translated by
Europeans and presented for Western readers.

History of the War in Bosnia during the Years 1737–8 and 9

Serving as a judge in his native Bosnia in 1737 when war broke out between
the Austrians and the Turks, Omer Efendi (about whose life little else is
known) produced this vivid account of the conflict from an Ottoman
perspective. Important for what it reveals about the region's social history,
the work was revised and published by Ibrahim Müteferrika (*c.*1672–1745),
the founder of Turkish printing. It was first published in English in 1830
after being translated by Charles Fraser, a professor at Edinburgh's Naval
and Military Academy. Fraser also added an introduction to the work that
gives both a brief history of Bosnia and an overview of the text. The narrative
begins with a description of the army of the invading Austrians, who are
described throughout as 'infidels'. An account is then given of the operations
of the war, through to the signing of the Belgrade treaty in 1739.

Cambridge University Press has long been a pioneer in the reissuing of out-of-print titles from its own backlist, producing digital reprints of books that are still sought after by scholars and students but could not be reprinted economically using traditional technology. The Cambridge Library Collection extends this activity to a wider range of books which are still of importance to researchers and professionals, either for the source material they contain, or as landmarks in the history of their academic discipline.

Drawing from the world-renowned collections in the Cambridge University Library and other partner libraries, and guided by the advice of experts in each subject area, Cambridge University Press is using state-of-the-art scanning machines in its own Printing House to capture the content of each book selected for inclusion. The files are processed to give a consistently clear, crisp image, and the books finished to the high quality standard for which the Press is recognised around the world. The latest print-on-demand technology ensures that the books will remain available indefinitely, and that orders for single or multiple copies can quickly be supplied.

The Cambridge Library Collection brings back to life books of enduring scholarly value (including out-of-copyright works originally issued by other publishers) across a wide range of disciplines in the humanities and social sciences and in science and technology.

History of the War in Bosnia

during the Years 1737–8 and 9

OMER EFENDI
TRANSLATED BY CHARLES FRASER

CAMBRIDGE UNIVERSITY PRESS

Cambridge, New York, Melbourne, Madrid, Cape Town,
Singapore, São Paolo, Delhi, Mexico City

Published in the United States of America by Cambridge University Press, New York

www.cambridge.org
Information on this title: www.cambridge.org/9781108055086

© in this compilation Cambridge University Press 2013

This edition first published 1830
This digitally printed version 2013

ISBN 978-1-108-05508-6 Paperback

Oriental Translation Fund

INSTITUTED 1828.

UNDER THE PATRONAGE OF

HIS MOST GRACIOUS MAJESTY

GEORGE THE FOURTH.

THIS COPY WAS PRINTED FOR

THE

ROYAL ASIATIC SOCIETY

OF GREAT BRITAIN AND IRELAND,

BENEFACTORS TO

THE

Oriental Translation Fund.

HISTORY

OF THE

WAR IN BOSNIA.

HISTORY

OF THE

WAR IN BOSNIA

DURING THE YEARS 1737-8 AND 9.

———◆———

TRANSLATED FROM THE TURKISH

BY C. FRASER,

PROFESSOR OF GERMAN IN THE NAVAL AND MILITARY ACADEMY, EDINBURGH.

———◆———

LONDON:

PRINTED FOR THE ORIENTAL TRANSLATION FUND.

SOLD BY J. MURRAY, ALBEMARLE STREET;

AND PARBURY, ALLEN, & CO., LEADENHALL STREET.

1830.

PRINTED BY A. J. VALPY,
RED LION COURT, FLEET STREET.

INTRODUCTION.

Bosnia, or Bosna, was included anciently in Pannonia Inferior; and in the fourth century formed a part of that vast district called Illyricum, which comprehended, under this general appellation, Rhætia, Noricum, Pannonia, Dalmatia, Mœsia or Mysia,* Thracia, Macedonia, and Greece; and which afterwards was divided into two provinces, viz. Liburnia and Dalmatia.

It received its present name from a river which runs through it to the Save (Savius), called Bosna (Bocantus); near the mouth of which stood Sir-

---

* In some histories Bosnia is supposed to be the country that was anciently called Mysia. Playfair, whom I follow, says: "That Mysia extended from the confines of Macedonia and Thracia northward to the Danube, and from Pannonia and Illyricum eastward to the Euxine sea: divided by the river Ciabrus, Zibris, into Mœsia Superior or Prima, now called Servia; and Mœsia Inferior or Secundus, now Bulgaria." Bosnia, or at least part of it, was, in 1103, called the kingdom of Rama.

mium, anciently the capital of Pannonia, and the residence of the Roman emperors when they visited the Illyrian frontiers; where Claudius expired. Budalia, eight miles above Sirmium, on the Save, 'was the birth-place of Decius; and Cibalis (Sivilet) about fifty miles above the same place, on the Save, was the birth-place of Gratian; near to which Constantine vanquished Licinius in 315.

The original inhabitants of these regions are represented as having been fierce and barbarous; painting their bodies with various colours, and subsisting by rapine and piracy. They attracted the notice of the Romans two centuries before the Christian era, and were finally subdued by Tiberius towards the conclusion of the reign of Augustus.

Modern Illyricum comprehends the countries which belonged to it in the middle age, and is divided into Hungarian and Turkish Illyricum. Bosnia, which belongs to the latter division, was in process of time annexed to the kingdom of Hungary, but was afterwards erected into an independent state, and governed by its own sovereigns from the year 1351* to 1465; when the Turks, under Mo-

---

* In 1389, Amurath I. in an obstinate engagement with the united armies of Bosnia, Servia, and Bulgaria, was slain by a Bosnian noble. A mausoleum was erected by the victorious army

hammed II., made themselves masters of it, about twelve years after the reduction of Constantinople. Stephen V., the last sovereign of Bosnia, was, on his surrendering himself, ordered by Mohammed, in violation of the most sacred promises, to be flayed alive: his family, and the nobles connected with him, were all sent to Constantinople to grace the triumphs of the Mohammedan conqueror. It is not improbable but this prince, urged on as he was by the most insatiable thirst of conquest, would have carried his triumphs as far as Imperial Rome herself, had it not been for the celebrated George Castriot, prince of Epirus, in Albania, generally known by the name of Scanderbeg, who with a small army resisted for many years all the power of the Turks, and gained twenty-two battles. He was at last obliged to take refuge in Lyssia, in the Venetian States, where he died in 1466; and with him also sunk the strength of Epirus, which afterwards became a Turkish province. Moham-

in memory of their king, and lamps are kept continually burning in it, which are watched by Dervishes. The Bosnian was put to death; and a stone has been placed over his grave, which is still revered by his countrymen. Fifty years afterwards, Amurath II. routed in the same place (the plain of Merles, or Cossovopoli, in Servia,) a Hungarian army.

med II. died in 1481, after having reduced twelve kingdoms and two hundred towns, and put to death eight hundred thousand Christians of both sexes.

Bosnia is bounded on the west by the Una, on the north by the Save, on the east by the Drin, which separates it from Servia, and on the south by a ridge of mountains, lying in 44½° N. latitude; being, according to some geographers, two hundred miles from east to west, and seventy-five from north to south, and according to others still less. Hassel estimates it to be 1062 German square miles, allowing the German square mile to be equal 11⅑ English square miles.

It forms one Pashalick, and is divided into three districts called Sanjiakships; viz. Banialuka, Orach or Orbach, and Serai. It is a mountainous country, containing some fruitful plains and valleys, and watered by many rivers which run northward to the Save. The oak, the ash, the poplar, the maple, the hornbeam, the aspen, and the birch, grow on the sides of its mountains; the summits of which are covered with larches, firs, and yews. A great navy, it is said, might be built of the timber in the forests. The late emperor of the French, aware of the advantages that might be derived from them, ordered tools to be forged in the country: and workmen were employed, by his direction, in cutting a road by which the French legions might penetrate into Illyria, and the Bosnian oaks be transported to the harbours on the Adriatic.

The author, or rather publisher, of the History of the War in Bosnia, has strictly confined his narrative to the operations of the war, and is entirely silent with regard to the state of the country and the amount of population, except that he says it was in a defenceless condition when the Imperial troops commenced their aggressions. He has not given us even a statement of the strength and condition of the towns and garrisons which were assaulted, or of the Mohammedan force which was mustered on that occasion, for the purpose of opposing the invaders of their country. He satisfies himself with describing the number and attitude of the enemy, and with delineating the prowess, the deeds of invincible valour and the success, of the " orthodox troops," though the number which are said to have been successively engaged in the various encounters with the enemy, seem in general to bear no proportion to the force which opposed them. He makes the Bosnians, the " true believers," not only to conquer the " execrated infidel wretches "—the Germans—at all points, but drive the Prince of Saxe

Hildburghausen from Bosnia, and, in conjunction with the Ottoman Imperial troops, the Duke of Lorrain and Count Seckendorff from Belgrade, the capital of Servia also.* In short, he records the defeat of the Germans to have been so very complete, that not a " hoof of them," as Ali Pasha, " the illustrious governor, prudent and skilful in affairs," expressed it in one of his military councils, was left behind. The Bosnian warriors were not content with the triumph of overpowering and expelling the enemy from their own territories, but, in their turn, carried devastation and death into the dominions of the enemy, beyond the Una:†

* When the imperial negotiators proposed a treaty of peace, the grand vizir, who commanded in person at the siege of Belgrade, replied in a manner which at once shewed the haughtiness and heroic firmness of the Turk: he asserted that the bad faith of Austria had been the sole cause of the war, wherein God had favoured the Mussulmans; and had espoused the just cause: " As there is but one God," he said, " I have only one word, and that word is Belgrade. Belgrade, untouched in its fortififactions, shall be restored to my sublime emperor, and for that price he will sign a peace."

† From the names of places given in the narrative, viz. Constanishæ, Ziren or Zrin, and Dūb, &c., against which the Moslems directed their hostility on this occasion, we can be at no loss to perceive, that Hungarian Croatia and Hungarian Dal-

and in all their battles and skirmishes, from first to last, they are not only victorious, but succeed also in carrying off immense booty, and in making many of the enemy prisoners, whilst they themselves are made to appear to have sustained very little loss.

Such is a short outline of the war in Bosnia, and we shall now leave Ibrahim to speak for himself. We are persuaded however, notwithstanding the defects we have been led to point out with respect to his narrative of the war; and we might still add, that the engagements, the scenes, and the heroes, are too much generalised to excite that interest, which a more succinct and detailed account would have awakened. It will yet be found both curious and peculiar, inasmuch as it is written by a Turk, who seldom writes; and also, as it gives a pretty full account, though not so circumstantial as

matia were the countries which are meant; and which have frequently been exposed to the ravages of Christian and Turkish troops. In the fifteenth century the Venetians reduced the whole of Dalmatia, but they have since been dispossessed of a considerable part of it. At present Hungarians, Venetians, Turks, and Ragusans, share it among them. Grasdankoi, a castle on the Una, was once the residence of the counts of Ziren or Zrin, and noted for its silver mine.

might be wished, of a war that was peculiarly disastrous to the Imperialists. The bad success of the
Germans may probably be ascribed to their having
at once divided their troops into five divisions, and
attacking Bosnia in five frontier points,*—a circumstance which gave the war the character of a skir-
mishing and partisan warfare, in which the Turks, it
is said, always shine. To this may be added the
advantages which the native possessors of the soil,
roused by every feeling which patriotism and reli-
gious hatred could inspire, must have had in repelling
a foreign invasion : so that the defeat of the Imperial
troops does not appear surprising.

Malte-Brun informs us that Bosnia is admirably
defended by nature ; that the roads are so very bad
that cannon or artillery can only be transported on
a few of them ; that the Turks, in the event of an
invasion, may convey the greater part of the provi-

---

* The first was directed against Banialuka ; the second against
the fortresses of Būzin and Chetin ; the third against Osterwitch-
atyk ; the fourth against Tzwernick, and the fifth against Yangibazar, or Novi-bazar. This last division reduced the fortress of
Niss in Servia on its march to Yangibazar. Niss is supposed to
have been the birth-place of Constantine the Great, and Pristina,
or Guisterdil, that of Justinian.

sions in Bosnia into their strong-holds; that the vizir can easily raise eighty thousand troops, thirty thousand of whom are sufficient for the defence of the forts, whilst the remaining fifty thousand may be employed in the campaign; and, in short, that the great difficulty in the conquest of Bosnia must be attributed to its numerous passes and thick woods, its castles, and also to the known courage of the Bosnians when they combat in their own land, and to the necessity of protecting an immense frontier against the incursions and attacks of light-armed troops.

The same author informs us further, that Bosnia is, in proportion to its size, more populous than any of the other provinces in European Turkey; and that it might, if its cultivation were extended, support three or four times the number of its present inhabitants: and in his table of the population in European Turkey, and which is constructed according to a scale of Hassel, (1823,) we find it stated that Bosnia contains five hundred and sixty thousand inhabitants. M. Liechtenstein, whom he quotes, calculates the population of Bosnia at nine hundred thousand individuals, of whom two-thirds are of Slavonian origin. Appended to this quotation from Liechtenstein is a note by Malte-Brun himself;

wherein he says, "I believe that M. Hassel and his guides have estimated the inhabitants of Bosnia and Servia too low by one half; and it is likely that the Slavonian population (including the Wallachians or Bulgaro-Slavo-Wallachians of Pindus) is at least equal to two millions."

Whichever of these statements may be the nearest to the truth, we may conclude that its population, when the Prince of Saxe Hildburghausen and the Duke of Lorrain led their mighty and well-appointed forces against Bosnia in 1736, was not a very great deal less than when the above statements were made.

In the history of the war in Bosnia we meet with the names of several places and fortresses which are no where else to be met with, but which, from their being mentioned in connexion with others that are known, may be conjectured to be somewhere in their neighbourhood, or at least not far from them. We shall endeavour to give a short sketch of some of the most remarkable places; and in doing this we shall take Malte-Brun for our guide, from whom we have already borrowed a considerable part of our information concerning Bosnia. We begin with Bosnia-Serai, now the capital of the country: besides which and other principal towns, there are, it is said, twenty-four fortresses and nineteen castles, which were built in the middle ages.

Bosnia-Serai contains a population not less than sixty thousand souls. The forts are each flanked by four small turrets, and the walls are twelve feet thick. The houses in the city are adorned with gardens. On all sides are minarets, bastions, and turrets, and the whole is surrounded by well-wooded hills watered by the Miliaska and other feeders of the Bosna. It may be concluded, from the extensive trade in arms and jewellery, Malte-Brun observes, and from the numerous caravans which pass to Constantinople, that the inhabitants are as industrious as any in the Turkish dominions. A third of the inhabitants are members of the Greek Church.

Traunick, formerly the capital of Bosnia, and by Ibrahim called the seat of government and jurisdiction, lies on the west of Bosnia-Serai towards the frontiers of Dalmatia. Its citadel, M. Desfosses says, is of little importance, while M. Petuisier says it is almost impregnable, It is the residence of the vizir-pasha of the province, on whom is conferred the title of the vizir of Hungary. His annual revenue amounts sometimes to 10,000*l.*; and all the offices enjoyed by the ancient courtiers exist still in the court of the vizir : but the guardian and protector, in the north-west of the empire is changed every three years, and is often, before that period expires, deprived of his dignities at the instigation of the Bosnians.

Yaitsha, or Iaicza, once the ancient abode of the kings of Bosnia, has fallen into decay.

Banialuka, a large and commercial town, is situated about twenty-four miles below Yaitsha on the Verbas. This is the only town of which any description is attempted in the following history. It contained, according to Ibrahim, forty temples and mosques ; but he makes no mention of the number of its population, leaving his readers to conjecture their probable number from their numerous temples. Malte-Brun says, that the houses, including those in the citadel, are not fewer than four thousand two hundred. The garrison is estimated at six thousand men, and the place is defended by three strong redoubts. The number of Christian families in it is about eighteen hundred.

Tzwernick, or Zwornick, situate on the Drin, had at one time a population of fourteen thousand souls, but at present it has less than six thousand. Vishegrade lies a little beyond it to the east. Maglay and Vrandouk, on the Bosnia, are remarkable for their strong citadels. Gradishka on the Save is one of the strongest places in the country, having been fortified, in 1774, by French engineers. This was the palanka which the Prince of Saxe Hildburghausen, on his entrance into Bosnia, first reduced; whence, also, he proceeded to Banialuka, where his troops not only met with a vigorous resistance, but were completely routed by the " orthodox troops," under the command of the vizir, Ali Pasha, and the intrepid Mohammed, the two principal heroes among the Moslems of that campaign.

The Sanjiakship of Orbach is not so well known as the other parts of Bosnia. Hadji Khalfah makes the population of the town of Fotschia, which lies in this district, to amount to ten thousand souls. The different writers who mention it are not agreed as to its situation ; some placing it on the White Drin, others on the Moracæ, and others again on the Zem. The church attached to the convent of Miloseva, in which are deposited the ashes of St. Saba, the first bishop of Servia, is said to be in this district. Yangibazar, or Novi-bazar, is in the district called Rascia, and is a populous town. Ozitcha, north of Yangibazar, was taken by the imperial troops in 1737, but was afterwards recovered by the Bosnians: it is a place of some trade, and contains about six thousand inhabitants.

Nooi or Novi, Dūb or Dūbieshæ, and Behack or Behka, are small fortresses on the Una, and which resisted, in 1789, the united efforts of an Austrian army.

Bosnia, before it was subjected to the Turkish yoke, was a Christian nation, though it is probable the inhabitants were split into Greek and Catholic Christians. Most of them have since, we learn, become Mussulmans, but differ entirely from the Turks in their manners, habits, and interests. Ibrahim has devoted a short but curious section, at the end of his work, to a description of the country and people of Bosnia, to which we refer the reader: their Christian neighbours are the members of a corrupt church. Those on the Drin and the Save, still attached to the Greek church, and those on the Verbas, from Yaitsha to Banialuka, and on the confines of Herzgovina, professing the doctrines of the Catholic faith, are all infected with the superstition, ignorance, and prevailing errors of the middle ages.

The Bosnian language is a dialect of the Servian, and generally spoken throughout the country. The Turks seldom think of acquiring it, and are considered strangers. Polygamy, so peculiar to Mohammedan countries, does not prevail to any great extent in Bosnia, and both sexes enjoy the privilege of choosing their companions for life. An unmarried female appears in public without a veil, and respect is shown to the mother of a family. In all these respects they differ widely from the inhabitants of eastern countries; and Malte-Brun says, " the barbarism of the Bosnians must be imputed to an intellectual separation from the rest of Europe : if they were enlightened,—if the Christian religion were preached in its gospel purity amongst them, they might soon become an independent nation."

We have now brought our observations on Bosnia to a close, and have only to say further, that in translating the following work, we have endeavoured to follow the original pretty closely, from an anxiety to preserve its oriental cast, which of course adds to its interest. The translation may, perhaps, from this cause appear clumsy and verbose, and not so well arranged as it might otherwise have been ; but we thought it would be injurious to sacrifice the raciness of the original in endeavouring to adapt it to European taste.

THE TRANSLATOR.

ACCOUNT

OF THE

WAR IN BOSNIA,

From the beginning of the *Muharram*, 1150 of the Hijra,
(April the 19th, 1737, A. D.) to the end of the month
Jamāda 'l avval, 1152. (August the 13th, 1739, A.D.)*

WHEN, by the will of God, the war broke out in
the eastern districts, and when several of the troops
which had been sent to aid the true believers, had
fallen a sacrifice to the greatness of the distance,
the badness of the water, and the unhealthiness of
the climate, it so happened, by the permission of
God, that the plague made its appearance in the
kingdom of Bosnia, and caused the destruction of
multitudes.

It was owing to the perfidious Muscovite infidels

---

* European accounts state, that hostilities began early in 1737,
and that the peace of Belgrade was signed on the 1st of September,
1739. A. D. The last day of *Jamāda 'l avval* fell on the 13th
of August, 1739. The date assigned in this work therefore appears to be sufficiently exact, as some days must be allowed from
the termination of hostilities to the conclusion of peace.

having violated their engagements with the Porte, that five thousand chosen men, standard-bearers, surgeons, and a number of brave officers, had been sent to the Russian frontiers, for the purpose of aiding the army of the faithful against the aggressions of the infidels. This circumstance left the kingdom of Bosnia in a great measure exposed, and also afforded an occasion to the infidel Germans to believe, that the country was in such a defenceless state, that they also were induced to violate the peace. Both Germans and Muscovites had formed, long before this, schemes against the peace and tranquillity of the empire ; and now both began to put their wicked designs into execution. Owing to the disasters which had befallen the empire in the east, these hateful wretches, the Germans, were led to think, when they perceived that Bosnia and the adjacent provinces were in a defenceless state in consequence of the war with the Muscovites, that the exalted Mohammedan power had become lax and feeble. They became inflamed with prospects of success, and wickedly resolved on attacking the Ottoman empire in various quarters. According to the account of the people of the country, their first object was to conquer Bosnia, and then the other provinces. The same account states, that more than a hundred and fifty thousand troops, from the German territory alone, came successively against Bosnia.

When the German and Muscovite emperors had formed their base intentions against the Ottoman

empire, as before hinted, they at the same time
deceitfully manifested an appearance of friendship.
The Muscovite, however, soon returned to his old
villany, whilst the Germans, with a hollow show of
good-will, continued to respect the existing treaty
of peace. The Porte, in consequence of this appearance of good understanding manifested by the Germans, was deceived ; and hence became less atten-
tive to the affairs of the frontiers on the west. The
Germans, however, no sooner perceived that the
army had been sent to the frontiers of Muscovy, and
that several provinces of the empire had been thus
necessarily deprived of military force, than they
forgot their engagements, seized the opportunity
which now offered itself, and determined on immediately entering the Ottoman frontiers. They commenced their operations against Bosnia* by dividing
the army, which was collected into five divisions,
each furnished with every thing necessary for the
war, and attacked it in five different places. The
first attack was directed against Banialuka.† Eighty
thousand Germans, and twenty thousand Hungarians, under the command of the Prince of Hildburghausen, and four other generals, were sent to
reduce the above place. At the distance of eight
hours‡ journey from this fortress, they threw several
bridges over the Save ; by which means they crossed

* See Preface.
† A fortified town on the river Verbas, about ten leagues south
of the Save.
‡ *An hour's journey* is about three English miles.

into Bosnia, and posted themselves in a palanka*
called Gradishka. The generals of the fortresses
Khurwàtbani, Copur, and Waradzin, with their dependencies, fierce as dæmons, divided their forces,
consisting of Germans and Croatians, into two
separate divisions, and marched against Buzin and
Chetin, two fortresses on the utmost confines of the
Ottoman empire. This formed the *second* grand
division of the enemy's army.

The *third*, a band of German and Lyka† infidels,
amounting to twenty thousand, under the command
of the generals of Lyka, Carloff, and Sang, planted
themselves before Osterwitch-atyk.‡

The *fourth*, an army of fifteen thousand Germans,
and as many Slavonians or Servians, and Hungarians,
made their way through the circle of Belgrade, and
fortified themselves in the vicinity of Tzwernik.§

The roads of Bosnia, Romeli, and Albania, being
almost entirely cut off by the enemy, they formed
the design also of taking possession of the main road
which leads to and from the interior of the empire to
Bosnia ; and therefore sent their *fifth* army towards

---

* Palanka (پلانکه) is derived from the Hungarian *plancæ*, and
means a petty fortress surrounded by palisadoes.

† Possibly the name of a particular body of Hungarian
troops.

‡ A little town with a castle, on the confines of Hungarian
Dalmatia.

§ Sometimes written *Zwornick*, a walled town defended by a
castle, on the Drin.

Yangi-bazar,* which is the key of Bosnia. On their way to that place they reduced the fortress of Niss. In this state of affairs it was next to impossible for the Islamite army to re-enter any of these places.

Thus was Bosnia not only nearly surrounded, but its total overthrow threatened by an immense horde of infernal firebrands, furnished with every sort of weapon and apparatus of destruction fit for that purpose. After they had fortified themselves in their various positions, however, and before commencing actual hostilities against Bosnia, they fixed a day on which the different leaders entered into correspondence with the German emperor, and agreed to proceed no further in their movements till they heard from him : and thus, for a time, they manifested hesitation and irresolution.

It was during this time, when the Muscovite violated the stability of the peace, and hastily employed his strength in injuring the country of the Osmanlis, and when the Germans commenced their aggressions against Bosnia, that the men of the frontiers, in such circumstances of doubt and perplexity, began to revolve in their minds these inauspicious appearances, and subsequently formed the plan of defending themselves and their country against the efforts of the enemy. The accounts which they had received relative to the way in which the enemy had collected, and how they were busily

* A town in Servia, a hundred and twelve miles south of Belgrade.

employed in building ships (or boats) on the Danube and the Save, were more than sufficient to excite their terror and amazement. The men of the borders, as well as the people of Bosnia, were universally plunged into a state of despair and distraction.

All these things, however, were not hid from his Excellency Ali Pasha, the august vizir, the governor of Bosnia. The vizir, expert in affairs, prudent, and incomparable, in order not to awaken or increase the perturbation of the people, or augment their perplexities, though he well knew the state of affairs, kept all his griefs and agitations within his own breast. From the very first appearance of these troubles, the illustrious vizir was full of care and anxiety as to the result, and carefully attended to them all ; so much so, indeed, that his thoughtful and agitated mind kept him, on many an occasion, from taking his usual rest either by night or by day. The distressing letters and petitions which were sent to him for assistance from the men of the borders, as well as those which were sent him from the other inhabitants of the kingdom, and the judicious answers which he ordered to be returned in reference to their urgent claims, are not forbidden to be touched upon in this work. I have laid a statement of the whole of these affairs before his Excellency the Prime Minister, and I am anxiously waiting for his Highness's commands ; and even the sentiments in some of the letters which have been sent from the royal camp, and which affirm that we are even now on good terms with the Germans, are not prohibited

being adverted to, inasmuch as they were intended
to soothe and allay the agitations of the people.

From other documents it would appear, however,
that it was after the German armies had come from
the inner provinces of their empire towards Bosnia,
and pretending for a time, as already observed, that
they had come with no hostile intention, that the
illustrious vizir became informed, by letters and
petitions from all ranks and conditions, of the real
state of affairs. This sad intelligence, it is said,
soon excited terror, and spread a mysterious amazement among the easy and undisturbed inhabitants
of Bosnia : it sunk them into the depth of surprise.
The vizir was no sooner apprised of this intelligence
than he made all necessary enquiry as to the actual
appearance of the enemy, and sent a special messenger to their infamous chief. The messenger lost
no time. On his arrival he represented to the chief,
in the name of the vizir, that the time specified in
the treaty of peace concluded at Puozeroff* with the
German emperor, had not then expired : and therefore wished to be informed why they had come with
such hostile appearance as they presented, and thus
awakening the fears of all the inhabitants of that
quarter, as well as threatening ruin and destruction
to the Ottoman empire. The hateful and cursed
commander replied : "We are not come with any
hostile intentions, or with any view opposed to the
good understanding and friendship which subsist

* It was at this place the famous treaty was concluded in 1718
between Charles VI. and Achmet III. It is usually written,
Passarowitz.

betwixt the German emperor and you. Though
we are come near to you," continued he, "it is only
with the view of guarding our own frontiers." The
messenger said in return : "How does it come to
pass, seeing there is no declaration of war, that it is
become necessary at this time, and in opposition to
established custom, that you should come here with
numerous troops and warlike stores?" The fierce
and execrable chief answered : "We have been so
enjoined : we do not know the reason of it. When
St. Peter's day (the 29th of June) arrives, you will
receive an answer." On finishing this sentence, he
gave such symptoms, in addition to the above
answers, as left no room to doubt any further of their
wicked and hostile intentions. The messenger
returned, and related circumstantially the whole of
his interview with the vile chief to the illustrious
vizir.

The vizir, after weighing all circumstances, saw it
was right to remain no longer inactive. Couriers
were immediately sent to all quarters, giving information of the state of affairs, and calling on the
inhabitants every where to prepare for resistance.
The grandees of state, the nobles, the enlightened
men of the frontiers, the judges, the mufti, the
priests, and the other learned effendis, were all
invited to assemble. This mandate they all promptly
obeyed by assembling in Traunick, the metropolis of
Bosnia. After they had all assembled together in
the governor's palace, his excellency the governor,
the illustrious vizir, entered immediately on the
business which had led to their convocation; and,

after saluting them all in the most respectful and appropriate terms, he proceeded thus: "Ere now you will all have learned that the Germans have collected themselves in large bodies on our borders, and that they appear prepared for commencing hostilities against our country. This was a kind of trouble which we did not anticipate, because we understood we were on a friendly footing with the German emperor; and still these wretches, the Germans, maintain a feigned appearance of friendly intentions and good faith. These inflamed and raging Germans, contrary to the treaty betwixt the German emperor and the Porte, have been collected from the inner provinces of their country, and are now within our borders. This German army has divided itself into certain divisions, and stands prepared for carrying their machinations against our country into effect. You are, besides, acquainted with the nature of the letters and petitions which have reached us from the rulers and commanders on our frontiers; and also with the message which was sent to the hostile chief, and the answer which he returned." The illustrious governor, after laying these things before the assembly, requested them to declare their sentiments, and offer their suggestions; "so that by this," said he, "it may appear how such weighty counsel and ardent patriotism may be considerately, properly, and correspondingly brought to have effect." The assembly took all these things into quiet consideration. The heart of each of them became cheerful to a great degree:

they continued their sittings; carefully weighed and examined the various and important propositions submitted to their deliberation, and entered fully into the views of the governor. The grandees noted carefully down, and put into form, all these transactions : and let it be observed, in justice to the illustrious governor, that it is owing to his judicious measures and consummate wisdom that our country was preserved, or rather delivered, from the movements and cruelty of the deceitful Germans ; that it did not fall, unprotected as it was, a prey to their ambition, by the stratagems which they had employed to overthrow it.

St. Peter's day (the 29th of June) was the day the enemy had determined on for commencing their work of destruction against Bosnia. It was therefore said in this assembly : " We are not ignorant of the fraud and deceit of the enemy of our faith. Let us be found ready and united, exercising complete foresight, and making every necessary preparation for meeting them with fortitude and valour. If the enemy commence their threatened hostilities, let us be found trusting in the arm of Omnipotence, and fleeing to Him for protection—let us hasten to the place where the enemy of our faith and of the empire first show themselves, and vigorously and manfully oppose them—let us, trusting in the all-avenging God, righteous and holy, quickly move against this hateful horde, and employ our utmost endeavour to oppose their assaults." When the governor understood these sentiments, coupled as

they were with just motives and determinations, he
applauded their wise decisions a thousand times;
congratulated them on their heroic determination,
and concluded with the wonted prayers, whilst
every heart exulted with joy at the prospect
of soon being called upon to fight for his country
and his faith. It was resolved in this assembly :
1. That the vizir, the nobles, and chiefs, having first
obtained the consent of the people, should begin
without delay to raise an army, and provide for its
being soon in a state fit for meeting the enemy, and
that persons qualified for taking the command should
be appointed : 2. That proper persons should be
selected for taking care of the infirm brothers and sons
of the men of Bosnia, who had gone to war against
Muscovy : 3. That it should be shewn clearly and
evidently why it became necessary that this warlike
attitude was assumed, in order that none might remain ignorant of the fraud and deceit of the enemy :
It was also resolved, in the 4th place, that all the
horse and foot, fit for the fatigues of war, should be
ready at a moment's notice, and repair to the plains
of Traunick.* This decree was ordered to be pro-
claimed throughout the kingdom, to the cities and
regions on the frontiers, and to all the ancient holders
of castles and passes; to the grand army ; and to all
the chief captains, lords, nobles, citizens, and inhabitants ; in order that all might be roused to vigilance and circumspection, and stand ready for
the purpose of repelling the enemy at the proper

* Situate on the borders of Dalmatia.

moment, and giving them battle. These strong and decisive orders were soon circulated every where, and warlike stores were ordered to be sent to the different districts. The governor and the states were employed in this way for a whole month, in making preparations for fierce contest and battle. The members of this assembly were quite determined ; and even those of them who had been disposed to give way to fear, became firm and resolute in the presence of the governor. The governor, after all these affairs had been fully attended to, permitted the members of the assembly to return to their respective abodes.

The various events which had recently taken place, both with respect to the appearance which the enemy had assumed, and the preparations which were deemed necessary for repelling him, caused much thought and anxiety of mind to the illustrious governor and to the inhabitants ; but more especially to him, as he felt particularly anxious as to how these events, hitherto concealed under a most mysterious Providence, might finally end. Being, however, in some measure provided with arms and other weapons of defence, they waited anxiously for the first movement of the enemy.

It was not long after these things that the day which the haughty and wicked infidels had mentioned arrived, on which they commenced their threatened movements against Bosnia. Their numerous army, now within the limits of the empire, began their work of bloodshed and death. These determined movements commenced on the very day they had fixed, viz. the 11th day of the third month (Rabīu 'l avval) 1500, but according to the European manner of reckoning, the 29th of July, 1737.*

The enemy of the faith, unfortunately, on the day above mentioned, took up a position in a place near to Tzwernik. Accounts of their having attacked a palanka in the neighbourhood of this fortress, of their killing the men, taking four hundred prisoners, consisting of women and children, and of their having seized and taken a great deal of plunder, and then burning the palanka, were soon communicated by the inhabitants of Tzwernik to the governor. These communications were accompanied by earnest petitions, soliciting the governor to send them, as speedily as possible, all the aid he was able to afford them. The illustrious governor was much afflicted by this intelligence. No other distressing event of this sort, however, had yet occurred: but this was a prelude to those which soon followed.

In this exigency, Okhurly Achmet Pasha, with

---

* July is an evident error for June, because St. Peter's day occurs on the 29th of June, and not on the 29th of July, as stated in the text. Now, as the first day of the Mahomedan year 1150 began on the 19th of April, 1737, it will be found that the eleventh day of Rabīu 'l avval fell apparently on the 30th of June in that year; making a difference of but one day from the time stated by the writer. But when we bear in mind that the Mahomedan day begins at the moment of sunset the preceding day, we shall find that the date assigned is quite correct.

all the men of his house and five *bairāks* * taken from the Janissaries of the court, was ordered to succour Tzwernik without delay.

Before this event took place, the governor and the head men of Bosnia, according to their previous resolution, had remained quiet, without offering any resistance to the invading army. On the arrival of the above intelligence, however, inactivity was changed into resolution and ardour. The illustrious governor, the noble vizir, without a moment's procrastination, pitched his camp in the plains of Traunick. Sheep, according to the rules of religion, were here sacrificed, and prayers were offered up for the divine assistance. Soon after this, the army of the empire made its appearance, and was ordered to repair to the governor's camp in the plains of Traunick. Orders to this effect were also sent to all quarters throughout the kingdom. In consequence of the sagacious and prudent measures which were adopted by the illustrious vizir, all the effective men of the different departments of the kingdom, with their chiefs; the learned effendis, the feudal chiefs, eager to fight; surgeons, and reverend muftis; all repaired to the camp of the orthodox believers at Traunick.

* Bairāk (بيراق), companies so called from their colours, or standards.

OF OSTERWITCH-ATYK.

The illustrious governor, full of deep contemplation and anxiety, was all eyes and ears, waiting for more information respecting the other secret arrangements and movements of the hateful enemy, in order more effectually to discover their strength and situation. So much was he pressed with thought, care, and agitation, as to the way in which he might most effectively render assistance to the orthodox faithful, and baffle the efforts of the enemies of the faith, that he was for several days and nights without taking any repose whatever. In this state of solicitude, and after several days, he at last learned that the enemy had advanced to Osterwitch-atyk on the 18th day of the month of the *first rabiu*,* and had erected a fortification before it.

OF THE ASSISTANCE RENDERED TO OSTERWITCH-ATYK.

The intrepid governor, wise and prudent, hastened, with all manner of solicitude and care, to afford them the necessary aid. He immediately ordered a reinforcement to be sent to Osterwitch-atyk; the command of which was committed to Ali Pasha

* The 6th of July, 1737.

Osman, chief of the royal messengers, and to the renowned and celebrated Mohammed, formerly commander of Tzwernik. This reinforcement amounted to five thousand men, all of them veterans of the most undaunted courage. The two commanders were enjoined by the governor to act in unison, and mutually to consult each other in their operations. The men of Traunick, and those in the country round it, composed this party; and the chief of the militia was also ordered to join himself to the two commanders. The commanders and their party of veterans set out for Osterwitch-atyk, a distance of thirty-three hours' journey; and the people of the country to which they went, when they saw an army was sent to defend their city and fortress, assembled in troops, and joined this army, and thus formed a considerable body of auxiliaries. The whole proceeded with hasty steps till they reached Belai, a place not far from the besieged fortress. Like the troubled confluence of two large rivers, which, after meeting and uniting into one,* make a tumultuous noise resembling the ocean; so these forces like the uplifted waves are in a state of ebullition to rescue the besieged Mussulmans.

* مرج البحرين (i. e. marju'l bahrain.)

OF THE AFFAIRS OF THE FORTRESS OF
OSTERWITCH-ATYK.

The enemy of the faith employed more than fifteen days in their efforts against this place, distressing its inhabitants night and day, but all their attempts—and they spared no means they could command to gain their object—were fruitless. In the fortress was a number of brave, resolute, and orthodox believers, who were ready and willing to risk their lives in their own defence and that of the place, and who were eager to fight the enemy; and by no means disposed to show them any compassion. There were in it, besides, a number of females who, like the ancient Bosnian women, acquired the courage of heroes. These changed their female dress for the habiliments of warriors, and appeared, sword in hand, in the ranks of the besieged, ready and determined, acting in concert with their male companions. Some of them carried balls, &c. to the fighting men, and stood ready for rendering any service they were able to perform. There were others who went forth with cups, jars, and other water-vessels, to meet their heroic bridegrooms, thirsting for the pure water of life,* and reminded them of the favour of God. Some em-

---

* I. e. immortality.—Paradise is the reward promised by Mohammed to those who fall fighting against infidels, and they are declared to be martyrs for the faith.

B

ployed themselves in preparing victuals, and others again administered medicine to the wounded, or bound up their wounds with suitable bandages. The troops in the fortress were indeed few in number, whilst those of the enemy were very numerous, and played night and day with their guns, &c. against the fortress: the inhabitants were thus sorely pressed, and were beginning to fear that the days of disgrace, of increasing distress, and of labour, were likely to be protracted: they also began to despair of receiving aid early enough to prevent their falling into the hands of the enemy. These were the circumstances in which they were when they wrote to the governor.

OF THE SUCCOUR SENT TO RESCUE OSTERWITCH-ATYK.

Whilst the inhabitants were thus situated, and perplexed about the troops, which they had heard had been sent to their aid, and whilst they were consulting together which was the surest method they could adopt for routing the enemy, just at this time the enemy suddenly raised the siege, and moved forward to meet the troops which were sent to succour Osterwitch-atyk, and who were now on their march from Belai. Both armies met, front to front. The Islamite army drew their swords, cried *Allah! Allah!* kept close together, and thus presented a formidable appearance to the enemy.

The champions of the faith lost no time in trying the bravery of the enemy, by falling on them with lion-like courage. It was not long before they perceived that the strength of the enemy began to give way. The brave men who joined the troops from the camp entered in among the enemy, brandishing their swords and spears, and made havoc in every direction. The victory was complete. Most of the enemy became food for the swords of the true believers, whilst those of them who escaped this carnage fled in confusion. The victorious warriors pursued these fugitives for the space of five hours, in which they hewed down numbers of them, and took many of them prisoners, whom they carried off in chains. The whole of their cannon and warlike stores was seized, besides a great quantity of plunder.

In this way, and by these means, Osterwitch-atyk was completely saved from the machinations of the execrated enemy. During these scenes, many of the brave Mussulmans, both men and women, departed from this vale of tears, and went to receive the rewards of martyrdom in the other world. Several were wounded, and others reduced to weakness in consequence of the fatigues which they had endured. The walls and the rampart of the fortress, and some of the most elevated dwellings in the city, were much injured by the cannon of the enemy. Some of the troops which had been sent to assist the besieged drank, also, the sweet sherbet of martyrdom: among whom was Osman Bey, one of the two commanders before mentioned. Of the infidel army, however, immense numbers perished. General Topal, the commander of this division of their army, was killed, and not one of their other leaders escaped either being killed or taken prisoner. Colonel Grooff was among the latter.

The victors, after this signal overthrow of the enemy, resolved on sending an account of their success to the governor, and appointed some of the intrepid warriors to be the bearers of this glorious intelligence, and also to carry along with them a few of the most eminent of their prisoners, and present them before him.

It must be observed, however, that the governor, after having sent off the reinforcement to Osterwitch-atyk, in consequence of hearing of the enemy's movements, and of the greatness of their numerical strength, was roused by his zeal and strength of obligations to afford more assistance, when necessary, and therefore he, his followers, and the whole of the Islamite camp, removed from Traunick towards Osterwitch-atyk. On the very day of the victory the governor commenced his march, and had proceeded no further than three hours' journey when he received intelligence of the joyful event. This news exhilarated the heart of the governor, and of the Mussulmans universally. After returning thanks to God, the illustrious governor ordered splendid presents to be made to the individuals who had brought him the joyful tidings, according to their rank and degree. The illustrious governor pitched his camp at a place called Yaitsha, six hours' journey further on.

OF THE ARMY WHICH WENT TOWARDS BANIALUKA.

The enemy's troops which had placed themselves at Gradishka, opposite to Banialuka, as before observed, continued for a time without offering any further hostility. At length, however, they destroyed that place, and marched towards Banialuka with the view of besieging it. Information of this having been communicated to the governor by the mufti of Banialuka, Mohammed Effendi, and other persons of distinction, it was soon resolved to send without delay aid to Banialuka, which was now threatened with a siege. The success, however, which had attended the Islamite army at Osterwitch-atyk gave a preponderance in favour of the Mussulmans, and served greatly to encourage them. There were present in Banialuka at this time, Agha Ibrahim, the Kāim Makām* of Serai, the Agha of the militia, with their followers, and a courageous party of the men of the borders; all of them inured to difficulties. The troops which were sent to succour this place reached their destination before the enemy had time to appear. Two or three days afterwards, the commander of the infidels, Prince Hildburghausen, while on his

* Locum tenens.

way from Gradishka, ordered a chosen party of seven or eight hundred men to proceed, under the command of Dubinel, a companion of one of the depraved friends of the emperor, the bastard of an infidel, to plunder and burn the city and its suburbs. This information having reached the inhabitants, it roused them and the garrison to rage and the desire of revenge. The citizens and the garrison met in one place; and after taking a view of the conduct of the enemy in entering the Ottoman dominions contrary to the existing treaty, their having burned a palanka belonging to it, their having killed the men who were in that palanka, and carrying off the women, and their attack on Osterwitch-atyk and other places belonging to the Porte, it appeared too notorious to leave them any longer in doubt of the hostile object of the enemy : their machinations appeared clear as day. When it was, therefore, proposed that every effort should be made to oppose the enemy, the lieutenant of the fortress and a number of weak-hearted men said, " We have been sent to take care of the fortress : we have received no orders to go to war. Is it, therefore, proper, in these circumstances, to proceed of our own accord ?" The multitude of the assembly, however, great and small, said in return, " The enemy is come to our doors. Last night they were within five or six hours' journey of our city : there is no doubt that they will be here either to-day or to-morrow. Is it not therefore imperative on us to oppose them ?" Ali Effendi, a native of Bosnia,

and a man of great bravery, and other doctors of
the law and observers of religion, all of them prudent and skilful in affairs, showed to a demon-
stration that, if the affair were allowed thus to continue in suspense, and not met immediately with
firmness and zeal, the consequence could not fail
to be disastrous to them all. Ali said further, that
they ought to be aware, lest through some sort of
temptation they should be led to cherish a feeling
of mercy for the hateful infidels. " There is no
doubt," said he, " that your slaughtered heroes,
your martyred saints, your pious labours, will be rewarded in both worlds." After saying this, he
lifted up his hand, pronounced a prayer, and then
said, " I have devoted you all "* (to God). This
speech had the effect of rousing them all to thirst
for conflict and battle.

At this moment of general agreement, eight hundred cavalry were selected from the city and fortress, and placed under the command of the Agha
of the militia, Mohammed Agha, who had been deputed by the governors, the commanders of Gradishka and Maglai, men of great bravery and
courage. Spies were immediately sent off to gain
information as to the state of the enemy.

In the meantime the eight thousand of the enemy
formerly alluded to divided themselves into three
divisions of *one, two,* and *five* thousand. They fell,
however, a few hours' journey backwards, in

---

* 1. e. to become martyrs for the true faith.

order that they might more conveniently concert matters as to their operations, and be the more able to render aid to each other when it should be found necessary to do so. This was their misfortune. The spies soon returned, and gave an account of their divided condition, and led the Mussulmans at once to perceive that the time had now arrived for taking revenge. The brave and heroic body of troops which had been chosen, as before observed, rushed out of the city about the *third* watch of the night, and by day-break came up to the lesser division, and prepared immediately for attacking it. The heroic and confederate Mussulmans, as the day advanced a little, drew their swords, rushed violently on the enemy, and scattered terror every where. The enemy, finding themselves unable to resist the impetuosity of the veteran Mussulmans, soon gave way. The greater part of them fell victims to the sword of the victorious warriors, whilst those of them who escaped the sword fled in precipitation to join the next greater division of their army. The victorious Mussulmans were, however, at their heels, and attacked this division also, with lion-like courage, exposing their own lives in the most heroic manner in this daring conflict with the execrated infidels. The victorious warriors succeeded in getting before this infidel host, and attacked them in every quarter. They were obliged to yield—their courage completely failed them— they turned their backs, and with cries of disorder fled from the victorious sword of the brave Mussulmans, and made towards the larger division of the army. In this mighty conflict only fifty Mussulmans fell, and about as many were wounded. On the part of the enemy, however, immense multitudes perished. A number of captains and one general were among their slain. Two captains, one of whom was the individual who was appointed to advance, and plunder and burn the city, were taken prisoners. Farhād Mustapha, a native of Bosnia, endeavouring to take the above mentioned general alive, the execrated wretch tried to destroy him by a ball from his piece. Mustapha directed his lance towards his breast: both fell off their horses and opposed each other with death-like fury; but Mustapha was the conqueror. When this infidel general was on the point of death, he opened his hateful mouth and asked the conquering Mustapha if there were yet many troops in the fortress. " Infidel," said the brave Mustapha, " what is that, henceforth, to either you or me?—Go to hell!" Immediately the hateful soul of the infidel made its way to the burning flames. The wounds of Mustapha, alas! were such as to admit of no cure, and he, in consequence thereof, was added to the number of martyrs who fell on this occasion.

The victorious Mussulmans, after obtaining these splendid victories over the enemy, returned in triumph to the city, and to the community of the true believers. After many expressions of joy and gratulation on the part of the inhabitants, it was agreed to send an account of these splendid achieve-

ments to the illustrious governor. Accordingly a
certain number of the delegated troops were appointed to this duty; and also to carry along with
them the two captive chiefs, and to present them
before him. The governor was still at Yaitsha when
the deputation arrived, which, without loss of time,
made known to him the nature of their embassy,
and presented the prisoners before him.

It was soon rumoured, however, that the remaining body of the enemy was making towards Banialuka. The governor, without delay, and with the
view of circumventing the enemy, removed his camp
to Puderashtasha, a distance of six hours' journey
from Yaitsha. Orders were immediately issued
every where for all the troops to meet on a certain
day, and at one hour of that day, in the Moslem
camp. After the troops which had been sent to
Osterwitch-atyk, and who had finished the war in
that quarter, returned to the camp, the governor,
after giving thanks to God for the success which
had attended them, made them splendid presents
as a reward of their victory. Other troops from
other places returned also to the camp.

The camp continued where it now was, and in
a state of quietness, till the danger which threatened Banialuka became more apparent. This no
sooner took place, however, than Mohammed, who
had been one of the victorious commanders at Osterwitch-atyk, was sent with a party towards Banialuka. Mohammed, after reaching the vicinity of
Banialuka, made every necessary observation, and

sent word to the governor how matters stood. The illustrious governor immediately sent him orders to retire to a place above Banialuka, on the Verbas, and there secrete himself and his men from the view of the enemy. Mohammed obeyed, but anxiously looked for the arrival of the governor and his army. The governor, however, was obliged to remain where he was for the space of fifteen days, waiting the arrival of the Islamite troops from the distant provinces, before which he was not in a condition to march to Banialuka.

In this interval, information reached the governor that the generals of Khurwatbani, of Waradzin and Copurwitchsha,* with their troops and an immense multitude of infidels, had formed themselves into two divisions : the first consisted of twenty thousand Germans and Croatians, and had besieged the fortress of Buzin, and the other division, consisting of an equal number, had besieged Chetin ; two places belonging to the Ottoman empire.

GOD, THE PRESERVER AND KEEPER OF LIFE!

This sad intelligence was as if the mighty ocean had roared, as if the contending depths struggled with each other. The venerable governor, the illustrious vizir, magnanimous and of high confidence in God, turned towards the Supreme Giver of all

---

* Places belonging to Croatia on the north of the Save.

good, and repeated over and over again the thoughts
of his heart before him. He and the honorable
commanders in the army entered into deep and
earnest deliberation and consultation, encouraged
each other, entered more fully into the bands of
amity and concord, and deliberated on the way by
which they might most effectually give help to their
friends and countrymen; and determined to maintain in this union and concord, the firmness of a
castle built on a rock.

The illustrious governor convoked all the members of his council, and laid before them the
accounts from the inhabitants of Buzin and
Chetin. In his speech before the council, he adverted to the success which God had given to their
arms at Osterwitch-atyk, and how the enemy was
there completely defeated. That was an event, he
observed, which brought them all much joy, "but
it is now," continued he, "succeeded by afflic-
tion, cares, and anxieties. Both these come to pass
by the providence of God. On one side Buzin and
Chetin (he still speaking) are besieged by the armies of
our enemies, and Banialuka is sorely pressed by the
siege which the enemy have also commenced against
it. In these circumstances how are we to act? and
which of our brethren in the faith are we first to
help?" The whole of the members of the council
bowed their heads, and became thoughtful. After
contemplating the communication which the governor had made to them, they awoke, as it were,

from a dream of surprise. They consulted together
on the various topics which had been laid before
them, and came, after due deliberation, to the unani-
mous conclusion, that though Buzin and Chetin cer-
tainly did belong to the Ottoman empire, yet they
were on the frontiers of Bosnia, whilst Banialuka
belonged to the interior; and that, although the
enemy should succeed in their attempts against these
places, yet it was their duty to recover the interior
of their country from the invading enemy. "When
this is accomplished," said they, "they would then
turn their arms to those quarters, and would not
leave a horse* of the enemy remaining within their
dominions." It was therefore agreed to, and resolved to succour Banialuka first. The governor
applauded this resolution, said that it was quite in
unison with his own sentiments, and promised that
the army should move towards Banialuka without
delay. After performing their devotions, in conformity to the rules of religion, the council broke up.

DESCRIPTION OF BANIALUKA.

Banialuka, at the commencement of the kingdom of Bosnia, was the residence of the governors
of Bosnia, and a strong fortress. The city and
suburbs contain at present forty temples and
mosques. A great river, the Verbas, runs through

* Literally, a hoof.

it; a branch of it touches the east side of the fortress, and runs along it. This river is navigable by ships: it is a great river: its source is in the district of Ak Kallah : rising among the mountains in that quarter, it runs from south to north ; reaches Yaitsha, passes through Banialuka, and falls into the Save, eight hours' journey from Banialuka. It is a fast-flowing and deep river. Ships laden at Banialuka are carried by it to the Save, and the Save carries them again to Belgrade.

THE ENEMY'S ATTACK ON BANIALUKA.

In the meanwhile the enemy, coming with all their forces, laid siege to Banialuka. They threw up a ditch around the fortification which they had erected against the fortress : they surrounded the city and fortress on the west, between the two branches of the river, with another large and deep ditch. The fourth part of their troops they made to cross over to the right side of the river, by two bridges which they had erected for that purpose : by the same means also they got over a number of field-pieces and other implements of war. They drew another large and deep ditch from the entrance of the city to the brink of the river : thus the city and fortress were surrounded by a cloud of oppressors, and circumvallated by injustice. The erections and ditches being completed, they opened their fire in

nine different places, using their utmost skill to beat
down the walls of the fortress. The inhabitants
became desperate, having night and day eighteen
hundred shot of various kinds poured in upon them :
the courageous followers of the prophet, however,
rushed forth occasionally in bands, and attacked the
enemy's batteries, cheering each other in their
daring attempts. Many of these brave men fell,
and many more were wounded; but greater numbers of the enemy perished. The army of the enemy,
however, was still strong and ardent in their work;
regarding neither the dead nor the living, they prose-
cuted it with their utmost vigour. The troops of
the faithful were not less ardent and zealous in
defending themselves against these infidels; they
opposed guns to guns, lead to lead, and slackened
not in their glorious efforts, but went on in their
work with heart and soul. It happened, however,
that a woman belonging to the faithful fell into the
hands of the enemy. The commander of the execrated infidels, when he saw this woman, thought
he might accomplish his purpose by her means: he
immediately wrote a letter, and sent it by her
to the fortress. The following is a translation of
the perfidious letter: "To the intrepid and devout
Pasha of Banialuka, and the other persons of distinction along with him, peace!—With this affectionate
token of our regard, and in conformity to good
amity, it is necessary to announce, candidly, to your
presently agitated minds, our views. You have
seen our warlike preparations, and contemplated the

strength of the imperial army. You too have performed many great deeds, it must be allowed ; you
have fully fulfilled your promises of fidelity. This is
enough—be it known to you, therefore, that whatever
zeal you may after this manifest, it will turn to no
good account. If you persist in your mad efforts,
you will foolishly perish in your attempts. You
have no force to contend with us. You will get
succour from no quarter : the pasha in whose succour you confide has only three thousand men ; I
have four illustrious generals with me, any one of
whom is able to brave the most renowned of your
pashas. Of what avail, then, will the coming of
your pasha be ? At this moment we have strong and
mighty armies besieging other fortresses of your
country ; the cheering news of their being victorious
is daily expected. Besides, the son-in-law of the
emperor, the Duke of Lorrain,* is appointed commander-in-chief of the imperial army, and all the
Ottoman provinces in Europe are already declared
to be vanquished. Only a few days ago he removed
from Belgrade, vanquished the fortress of Niss,† and
is now on his march to the fortress of Widdin.‡
Special messengers have brought me letters informing
me of all this : if you wish to see them, I shall send

* Successively the husband of Maria Theresa, and emperor of
Germany.

† A walled town, situate on a river of the same name, about
fifty leagues south-east of Belgrade.

‡ A fortress on the Danube, in the north-east corner of Bulgaria, and upwards of forty leagues south-east of Belgrade.

them to you, and you will be convinced: you see you have no alternative left : at all events we will take the fortress ; then nothing will remain to you, if you continue obstinate, but ruin to yourselves and conflagration to your city and fortress. It remains, therefore, with you to decide which of these alternatives you will adopt; if you accept of our advice and timely warning, we shall send you in safety with your acknowledged property to any place you choose ; if, however, you reject our proposals and continue obstinate, we shall utterly destroy you :—do not say, therefore, that you have not had due notice.—Peace !"

This malicious and deceitful letter was read to the people, from the contents of which it appeared but too evident, that by their protestations of friendship they meant to convince them that they came to do them good. This letter was no sooner read in the presence of the people, however, than the pasha of the fortress said, in the presence of the whole assembly : " People of Mohammed, fathers, brothers, children, you have heard the vain-glorious boastings of these infidels ;—what do you say ?" They all in return said : " This fortress belongs to his majesty, the magnificent, the powerful, and glorious asylum of protection, the emperor of the Ottomans : we will never with our hands give it over to the enemy : we, with our families, have lived under the wing of its protection : the place of our fathers we will not yield to the enemy of our faith : we are ready to sacrifice our lives in behalf of our religion and our emperor; none of us, except he perish, will withdraw his hand from the sword." These solemn resolves were again repeated over the holy book, when all shook hands, and each went away, thus inspired, to his respective place. They all agreed, however, to give reason to the enemy to believe that they had accepted of their proposals, and fired off their guns.

The pasha that same night wrote letters to the governor, intimating to him the state of affairs, and sent them by men well acquainted with the roads and by-paths. These men having disguised themselves, approached secretly the enemy's works about the first watch of the night, crossed the ditches unobserved, and arrived in safety at the governor's camp. The governor having read these letters, wrote in return, and assured them of aid, and in his consummate wisdom encouraged them to be zealous, and made them promises of reward : "when behold," said he in his letter, "I personally, and a complete and zealous army, are ready like the raging sea to come to your assistance. By the help of God I will soon reach you." This heart-cheering letter was sent off the following night by the above messengers. Before dispatching these messengers, he told them to take different routes, in order that they might escape being observed; by the help of God, however, they reached the fortress in safety, having taken the same road by which they went, and crossing the enemy's ditches as before, without having been observed by any of them. The intelligence which they carried from the governor excited their courage, and filled them with joy and hope.

The governor in the meantime made all preparations : and on the 23rd of the month *Timuz** (July), he moved with his camp from the place where it was pitched by break of day, with pomp and great glory, directly towards the enemy. When he was about three hours' journey forward, he, in conformity to a plan previously formed, turned from the high road, and marched along the side of the hills near Banialuka, towards the Verbas. The renowned Mohammed on the same day left the place where he had secreted himself, and in three hours' march reached the Verbas : and having crossed it with his men, consisting of foot and horse, he took up a position on a high hill above Banialuka, having that day performed a journey of twelve hours. Next day being market day, he descended at two o'clock into the plains of Banialuka, and formed soon afterwards a conjunction with the governor's army. In the meantime the reverend and august governor, the commander-in-chief, was in a state of complete readiness, exercising the most consummate skill in all his operations ; having in his train the Agha of Serai and the royal Janissaries. The lord of Bosnia, the cream and the felicity of the state ; the effendis of the various departments, the judges, the inhabi-

---

* The mention of *Timuz*, a Syrian month, which is indisputably July, supports the note already made p. 13, that the 29th of July had been put by error for the 29th of June.

tants skilled in affairs, and heroic officers, sat together in council, and afforded to the commander-
in-chief their counsel and advice. The troops under
Mohammed formed the right wing; and the militia
and the standard-bearers, with their new auxiliaries,
formed the left. The whole Moslem army was thus
in an attitude for commencing the battle with either
the right, left, or middle divisions, as circumstances
might seem to require. A number of others, such
as preachers, priests, &c., hastened to join themselves to the Moslem army, in order to take a part
in this honourable war. Others, in the meanwhile,
employed themselves in performing pious duties,
offering up various prayers, &c. &c., and in imploring
direction of God in the mysterious difficulties with
which his divine will had surrounded them. In
this state, and thus animated and prepared, they
commenced their movement, though slowly, towards
the field of battle. The commander-in-chief, when
they were within a short distance of the field, stepped
forward to the front, and delivered to them a speech
suitable to the circumstances in which they were
placed; saying to one " Father," to another " Son,"
to a third, " Brother,—this is a day of vengeance.
This day I am as one of you, I am nothing more
than a poor humble servant of God. This day is
a day in which we are willingly to offer ourselves
sacrifices in behalf of our great, illustrious, benevo-
lent, merciful, native lord, the Ottoman emperor,
under whose wings we have taken refuge, and in
behalf also of our religion." In this way did the

commander-in-chief prepare the minds of his orthodox army, for meeting with patience and calmness
the fierce battle and contest which was soon to
ensue. After having animated and encouraged his
troops, he returned to his place, whilst his camp
presented a picture of glory and strength, of firmness and union.

The execrated enemy did not imagine that the
Moslem army had crossed the river, till they saw
the troops of the faithful coming down upon them
from the hills, which caused immediately great com-
motions and stirrings amongst them, both in the line
of their fortification and in their trenches: fifteen
thousand more troops came to this side of the river,
and joined themselves under four generals, to those
who had been sent thither before: their cannon
they pointed at the Moslems; and two divisions,
trusting to the fate of fortune, were placed to oppose
the army of the faithful : the night coming on, however, put a stop to any further proceedings on both
sides.

Next day the pious and affectionate commander-
in-chief descended from his horse and touched the
base earth with his face, weeping and saying, "O
God! O God! this is a day of slaughter,—a day
mocking, as it were, the honours and destructions of
the day of judgment. Do not put thy servant to
shame ; shew compassion this time also to thy un-
worthy servant, for the sake of the true religion and
the chief of the prophets (Mohammed). My intentions are according to law and justice : it is the work

of the infidels to obliterate the glory of the true
faith from the page of the world, the pure attributes
of God from the face of the earth, and to drive away
the belief of the necessary existence and the excel-
lence and glory of the One God. My supplication
is, that God may defeat and destroy these faithless
and treacherous wretches, who have wickedly and
deceitfully attempted to ruin thy humble servants."
After having put up these humble prayers to God,
he mounted his steed, drew his sabre, brandished it
before the enemy, and, after giving a sign to his
troops to commence their attack, he rushed forward
to battle. The orthodox army, like the mighty
waves of the ocean, moved from their place, crying
Allah ! Allah ! and without regarding the cannon and
fire-arms of the enemy, entered into close contest
and battle with the hostile army and enemies of the
faith. The orthodox army, by the divine assistance,
was soon successful in destroying four of the enemy's
positions, and succeeded also in slaying three of their
principal generals. A great number of these abject
wretches became terror-struck, and whilst trying to
escape by flight, fell into the river and were drowned.
During two hours' struggle, in which the Moslems
were victorious, many of the infidels were cut
down : they succeeded, however, though with difficulty, in getting a reinforcement from the other
side of the river, and, being still numerous, they
seemed determined to continue the contest, regarding
neither the living nor the dead ; but in the space of
four hours more they were obliged to give way.

The roar of the cannon, and the brandishing of swords and javelins ceased. It is related that Mohammed, who commanded the right wing of the Moslems, had his horse shot under him a little after he had entered into the battle, but immediately mounted another which his servant brought him : this was also shot ; but the ardent and zealous *Capudan** mounted a third, which he seized from another of his servants. Entering within the lines of the enemy, and scattering death around him, this new horse fell, and he himself was wounded. In these circumstances of adverse fortune, and though on foot wounded, and his head streaming with blood, he did not permit the enemy to make him their prey. It is further said of him, that when he was brought into the presence of the commander-in-chief, a fine and splendid steed, a garment of honour, and a wreath of glory, were presented to him, besides many other things, as tokens of esteem and respect.

No sooner, however, did the intrepid *Capudan* Mohammed get his wounds bound up than again he mounted on horseback, entered the ranks against the enemy, and did wonders. The broken and enfeebled enemy was no longer able to oppose the impetuosity of the orthodox troops, who were everywhere victorious. The favour-bestowing banners of Islam returned from this carnage with great pomp, and the troops with demonstrations of joy at the

* Corruption of captain.

splendid victory they had achieved. In this dreadful second conflict many of the blessed Moslems, in their zeal for the faith, passed from this vain world to a place in Paradise as their inheritance. However, the multitudes of the infidels who perished by the victorious swords of the faithful were innumerable. The field of battle was covered with slaughtered unbelievers. Their celebrated commander and general fell also, and his soul went to perdition.

Thus, by the guidance and protection and favour of Heaven, the orthodox faithful vanquished completely the power of the enemy, which afforded them joy and exultation and triumph. It is conjectured that this famous battle commenced three hours after sun-rise on one of the days in the month of July, and continued till the sun was half west. If this account be correct, the orthodox must have contended with these abject wretches for more than five watches. In their last attack on the enemy they were so completely successful, that they drove them to seek retreat by the bridges, but which had been cut down before they could reach them, and thus they nearly all perished in the Verbas, except about two hundred of them who succeeded in swimming across. On this glorious day the Mussulmans took twelve pieces of cannon, three mortars, more than two thousand three hundred tents; fifteen hundred barrels of powder; numberless muskets, swords, and spears; provisions, cows, sheep, waggons, &c. &c. &c. In consequence of the

bridges being cut down, they were not able to pur-
sue their victory any further; but the remainder of
the enemy, when night arrived, left their fortification
on the opposite side of the river, and fled along the
Save, by which they had come. Before next morning,
however, the bridges were repaired, when the victorious veterans went in pursuit of them, and soon overtook them in their flight. During this pursuit,
which continued for about three hours, many of
them were killed, and many more were taken prisoners. So great was the extremity to which they
were now reduced, that those who had escaped the
sword supplicated with tears, saying: " Oh, if you
know or acknowledge the God of the Ottomans,—if
you love your Mohammed, show us mercy!" The
true believers, after perceiving this confession of
guilt, and it being the peculiar province of the true
religion to forgive injuries and show compassion to
the unfortunate, restrained their hands, and permitted
them to make the best of their way with impunity.
The entire destruction of these enemies was fully in
the power of the faithful, and it grieved them not a
little afterwards that they did not utterly destroy
them. The number of the enemy has been called
in question, but according to the account given
by the prisoners who were taken, the number that
came against Banialuka amounted to eighty thousand. These, with about twenty thousand German peasants, who followed the chances of war,
with the view of possessing themselves of plunder
taken from the Bosnian peasants, amount in all,

according to the computation of the enemy himself, to one hundred thousand.

OF THE SLAIN.[*]

By the help of the Most High God, and according to the rules of religion, the *first* thing which was attended to after the discomfiture of the enemy, was to look after the martyrs who fell on this occasion, both inside and outside of the fortress, on the ramparts, in the city and suburbs, and elsewhere, besides those who fell in the field of battle, and to bury them in conformity to the rules of the Koran. Before committing them to the dust, the prescribed prayers were repeated over their dead bodies. In the *second* place, persons were appointed to separate the bodies of the faithful from those of the infidels which were lying on the field of battle and on the river side, and buried them with their clothes on after the customary prayers had been repeated over them. The venerable governor was present during the whole of the time the prayers were offering up.

OF THE WOUNDED.

Every thing was done for the wounded that could be done : some were allowed to return home for a time, whilst women, acquainted with the art of healing, were forward to render them all the assist-

---

[*] They are styled martyrs in the original.

ance in their power. Those belonging to the city and fortress were accommodated with suitable and comfortable places provided for them. The spacious palace belonging to Prince Mustapha of that place, after it was cleared out and fitted up for an hospital, received twelve hundred wounded into it.

THE THANKSGIVING OF THE DIVAN.

In consequence of the signal victory obtained over the infidels, great rejoicings took place. The camp of the infidels became that of the faithful. The day after the victory, the victorious commander-in-chief held a council on the spot where the victory was obtained. The whole community of the faithful met and congratulated each other on their late successes, humbled themselves before God, made confessions, &c. &c., and offered up prayers and praises to God. All the inhabitants, the garrison, the captains of castles, the chief lords, nobles, officers, men-of-war, judges, priests, orators, &c., celebrated the victory in a manner suitable to the occasion; they lauded the illustrious and victorious governor, and kissed the hem of his garment, in honour of his splendid victory. The brave and valiant commander-in-chief turned and said, " May all your wars be prosperous!"— then, casting a gracious look on all around him, ordered splendid presents and garments of honour to be distributed, and spoke in a strain calculated to fill them with joy and gladness. The warriors in the governor's camp, the nobles, officers, and captains from the frontiers, besides the wise and learned effendis from the different departments, who had joined themselves to the governor's camp, came all forward and expressed their admiration of the governor, and also their gratitude for the great actions which he had performed. The illustrious commander-in-chief turned himself to them and said, after blessing them and wishing them all happiness and prosperity: " May your faces be white!" (i. e. May you be happy, or blessed.) After uttering this prayer, he with his own hands made distribution of his favours, according to their respective merits and degrees of rank. It is related by an undoubted friend, that the two thousand *chelengs** which had reached the camp on this occasion were not sufficient for the distribution which the governor made, and that he broke up the silver vessels which he had by him, and scattered abundance of *chelengs* amongst his troops.

OF THE REPAIRS OF THE FORTRESS.

After the affairs of the garrison, and the necessaries requisite for the fortress were arranged, an order was issued for repairing the injuries the wall, battlements, and high buildings had sustained by the vil-

---

* *Cheleng* (چلنك). This word seems, from the way it is applied throughout the book, to signify an ornament for the head.

lainous enemy, and which, after some days that were employed in celebrating the victory, were brought to a happy conclusion.

OF THE FORTRESS OF BŪZIN.

Whilst the governor and his zealous army of faithful believers were at Puderashtasha, he received information of the fortresses of Būzin and Chetin, belonging to the frontiers of the Ottoman empire, being besieged by the enemy as before observed. The execrated guardian of Croatia, with an innumerable army of infidels, marched to the fortress of Novi, on the frontiers of Bosnia, with the view of taking it; but, in consequence of the rivers Una and Sana being at that time impassable, he spent forty days in the vain expectation of being able to get across these rivers, and accomplish the reduction of that place. Enraged by this disappointment, he proceeded towards Būzin, about eight hours' journey north-west of Novi, and commenced the siege of that fortress. Although the inhabitants of this fortress were few in number, they manifested the greatest courage and firmness in defending themselves and their place; their women, also, acting like their husbands, were no less courageous and valiant. The deeds which they performed, and the courage which they displayed in repelling and defeating the enemy, have been recorded in the language of the noble and ignoble of the kingdom of Bosnia.

Some few days after the commencement of the
siege, the inhabitants, in order to inform the governor, the illustrious vizir, of their circumstances, sent
off by night the flag-bearer Ahmad, and a few others
of undaunted courage, with their petitions. As the
governor's camp at Puderashtasha was twenty-six
hours' journey from Būzin, the messengers made
great haste, and fortunately fell in with his troops
as he was on his march towards Banialuka. As the
illustrious governor had however determined on rescuing Banialuka, and therefore required all the troops
he had with him, he immediately issued orders for
the troops in Novi, Behka, Karupa, and Ostruwishsha,
to assemble, and one division of them to repair to
his camp before Banialuka, and the other to proceed to the aid of Būzin and Chetin. The exalted
governor in the mean time gave Ahmad many as-
surances and promises, several presents as tokens of
respect, and sent him away with secret instructions.
Ahmad returned in safety to Būzin, and encouraged
the hearts of the inhabitants, by telling them that
the noble pasha himself, and his innumerable army,
would soon come to their relief, and perform wonders in their behalf. " In the meantime," said he,
" let us be zealous till the commander-in-chief, with
his victorious army, arrive ; let us not bring reproach
on ourselves by being cowardly." On one or two
occasions he went out of the fort by night, and made
towards Osterwitch, and encouraged the men of
that place also, saying : " When the inhabitants see
you are ready and determined, they will be encou-

raged to hold out : be ye all, therefore, all eye
and ear :—behold, his excellency the pasha will cer-
tainly come to your relief—be under no solicitude
whatever about that." Thus did he so entirely inspire them with courage to hold out against the
enemy, that he returned to his own fortress. In so
very masterly a manner did he carry on his measures,
that he completely prevented the enemy from perceiving the weak state in which they were, and by
this means prevented the fortress from falling into
their hands. Ahmad also communicated through
fit persons with the fortress of Chetin, and succeeded
in bringing its inhabitants to the same views and
determination ; so that truly this man, by his stratagems, was the means of rousing the inhabitants of
these different places to courage and resistance : in
short, although the enemy had expended fifteen days
in trying to reduce Būzin, they did not succeed,
which was entirely owing to the stratagem practised
by Ahmad.

In the meantime the news of the defeat of the
infidels at Banialuka reached Ostruwishsha, a distance of six miles from Būzin. This glorious event
was the cause of much joy to them all. Not willing
to wait any longer for the arrival of the governor, a
party of veterans set out immediately for the purpose of rescuing Būzin from the efforts of the besiegers. Although the infatuated enemy was made
aware of the fate of their brethren at Banialuka, yet
so were they driven on by fate that they brought
ruin and defeat upon themselves also. They no

sooner saw the orthodox troops drawing towards them than they became confounded and fled. The troops of Ostruwishsha, joining themselves to the veterans of Būzin, fell upon these execrated wretches, and made great havoc amongst them. Many of them they slew with the edge of the sword; many more of them were made prisoners; and the whole of their baggage, besides several pieces of cannon, fell into the hands of the victorious Moslems.

OF THE FORTRESS OF CHETIN.

The inhabitants, the men-of-war, and the women, of this fortress, encouraged and strengthened each other in their determination to oppose the enemy. In the hope that the governor would soon come to their assistance, they endured patiently the calamity of the war in the bravest manner. Their resistance was not in vain; for no sooner did the news of the defeat at Banialuka and that at Būzin reach the infidels, than they all turned their backs and fled in tumultuous confusion. The troops which had gone to assist Būzin, the people of Chetin, and those in the country round about, went in pursuit of these fugitives, and succeeded in taking several of them prisoners, besides taking a great deal of plunder.

The events which had taken place at Būzin and Chetin, when communicated to the illustrious governor, awakened in his mind, and in the minds of his followers, unmingled joy. This happy intelligence was brought to the governor by Ahmad, whilst he was yet at Banialuka. The governor, in consideration of Ahmad's important services, conferred many tokens of respect upon him, and raised him besides to the command of a body of cavalry.

THE REMOVAL OF THE MOSLEM CAMP FROM BANIALUKA.

As the foundation of an impregnable castle had been commenced a considerable time before in the city of Serai, and as the aggressions of the enemy were apparently put a stop to, the governor, instead of crossing the frontiers, removed without any further delay to Serai. This movement commenced on the Sabbath-day (Saturday), the 13th of the last *rabia*,* when he passed through Traunick, and reached Serai in peace and safety. The foundation and the building of the castle being finished, the necessary apparatus for this new place of strength was accordingly furnished, and every thing was put in proper order.

OF THE TAKING OF YANGIBAZAR BY THE ENEMY.

When, as before observed, the enemy had removed from Belgrade, they went along the banks of the Danube as far as Pūzerūksha, where they crossed

* The 31st of July, 1737.

D

the Danube by bridges which they had erected,
having taken along with them all the troops they
could find about Temeswar. They formed themselves into two divisions, and pressed forward under
the command of the Duke of Lorrain, son-in-law of
the emperor, towards the fortress of Niss, which they
soon reduced. Niss had no sooner fallen, than he
ordered a troop to proceed to Yangibazar, which is
the key of Bosnia in that quarter. The inhabitants
of Yangibazar, having heard of the approach of this
infidel horde, became terrified, and fled to the top of
a mountain, where they fortified themselves. In the
meantime the enemy made themselves masters of
this fortress. After the enemy had taken a place
of so much consequence to Bosnia, the inhabitants,
i. e. those who fled at the approach of the enemy to
the top of the hill, were induced, through the instrumentality of some of the Albanians, who made them
promises, to submit themselves to the enemy of the
faith, and afterwards joined them against the faithful. Thus the road entering into and leading from
the kingdom of Bosnia was completely cut off.

THE RETAKING OF YANGIBAZAR.

When information of these things reached the
reverend and august governor in the city of Serai,
the chief of the stewards, Agha Yākūb, the chief of
the royal messengers, Agha Mohammed, and Pasha
Murād Beg, set out immediately with their respec-

tive men and a party able to use arms, with the
view of attacking the infernal firebrands who had
taken Yangibazar. This gallant troop, by the divine
assistance, soon rescued it out of the hands of the
infidels. After clearing the road to and from Bosnia
of these reptiles, they turned their arms against those
traitors and rebels who had assisted the enemy,
killed several of them, took their women and
children captives, seized a great deal of spoil, and
then returned to the city of Serai.

THE FORTRESS OF OZITCHA.

After the enemy had reduced Niss, as before
observed, they sent a troop of fifteen thousand infidels to attack the fortress of Ozitcha. When information of this event reached Serai, it happened that
the greater part of the troops had just been dispersed
into quarters. Couriers were immediately sent off
in all directions, requiring the troops of the faithful
to re-assemble in the plains of Glaasansha; to which
the illustrious governor soon repaired in person, and
where he pitched his camp. After remaining at
this place for a certain time, in order that the troops
might assemble themselves, he moved with his camp
to a place called Asamsha. Here he made himself
acquainted with the state of affairs and the condition

---

* Eight leagues south of Yangibazar, near the frontiers of
Bosnia.

of his brave troops, and afterwards held a council of
war, in which it was resolved unanimously, that the
governor, the illustrious vizir, should send a sufficient number of troops to aid the besieged. Accordingly a chosen band of between five and six
thousand got secretly into a village in its neighbourhood : the well known Mohammed, who fought so
bravely at Banialuka, was appointed to be their
leader. Mohammed crossed the river with his men,
and hastened towards the fortress : but before he
could reach the place, the frightened inhabitants,
seeing no mode of delivery, and viewing themselves
as ruined if they continued any longer to resist,
gave themselves up to the enemy after a few days'
siege, on the condition of being allowed to depart to
some other place. The enemy, in conformity to
their wishes, sent them away under an escort of two
captains and one hundred and thirty Germans, to
the place they had signified. With this party
Mohammed met, as he was making towards the
fortress, and took them all prisoners, and brought
them to the governor's camp, and presented them
before him, and awaited his commands. The illustrious governor, after weighing all circumstances,
and particularly the giving up of the fortress to the
enemy, immediately ordered the two commanders,
Haji Ismael and Nāib Mustapha, to be put to
death in the presence of the Germans, and punished
the rest for their cowardice. Suitable lodgings in
the meantime were provided for the Germans in the
camp, and they were otherwise hospitably treated :

and Mohammed was again dispatched with his five
or six thousand men for the purpose of recapturing
the fortress.

After a delay of two days, the Germans were
permitted to depart, the governor allowing cloth for
a garment to each of the two captains, and a piece of
gold to each of the men.

Mohammed, in the meantime, arrived before the
fortress. Although this fortress was firmly constructed, and every way in a good condition when it
fell into the hand of the enemy, yet the Moslem
troops, though they had neither cannon nor maga-
zine by which they might operate against the enemy
now within it, soon overpowered the five or six
hundred Germans and other worthless infidels who
were in it, and killed them ; taking more than a
thousand women and children captives. After
clearing the country every where around of these
infidels, they returned to the camp with great spoils.
The fortress of Ozitcha was again repaired and put
in a fit condition, whilst the governor and his men-of-
war were upon the alert as to the next appearance
the enemy might make, and ready to fall upon them
like an overflowing river.

As tranquillity was again restored, and as the
governor remained undisturbed in his camp, it came
to pass that the communication by letters from the
grand vizir in the imperial camp having been cut off,
became a subject of conversation among the people,
as well as of wonder. The august governor, by his
sublime prudence and foresight, hastened immedi-

ately to quiet and allay the uneasiness and agitation of the people. The governor appointed the renowned Mohammed to proceed with a hundred and twenty courageous followers towards Belgrade, in order to discover the state of the enemy which occupied Niss. The brave Mohammed, with his no less brave associates, left the camp in the darkness of the night, crossed the Drin, and when they were four hours' journey from Ozitcha, after passing by it, they arrived at Palanka, on the road to Belgrade, which had been destroyed. In coming to this place they met with a troop of Hungarians, whom they immediately attacked, killed fifteen of them, and carried eight of them prisoners to the Moslem camp. The governor was so much overjoyed, that he presented a robe to Mohammed with his own hands, and placed a gold wreath on his head, making at the same time suitable presents to his brave associates, and extolling them to the skies.

The infidel troops, under the command of the emperor's son-in-law, took Niss without resistance. A general of the name of Alexander, with a considerable body of Germans, were garrisoned in it. The account which was current, and was related by some of the enemy's soldiers, relative to this transaction, is this: "The son-in-law to the emperor determined on entering Bosnia from Niss; to cross the bridge of Wishœgrad, and push directly towards Serai, it being almost, it was believed in his camp, without any sort of fence or fortification. With these views he waited anxiously for a courier from

Vienna. We were sent to this quarter in the meantime, where we carried on plundering for some time.
The army at Niss, after we left it, was divided into
two divisions. One of these divisions was sent towards Widdin, and the other proceeded, under the
command of the son-in-law of the emperor, to Ozitcha, where he made enquiry concerning the governor
of Bosnia." According to the account of the people
of Ozitcha, the Germans, who had been two days in
the governor's camp, told him that " the governor
of Bosnia is encamped in a place called Asamsha,
eight hours' journey off; has an army of more than
a hundred thousand choice troops : he knows of
your intentions against Serai. When the emperor's
son-in-law heard this, he relinquished his object,
followed the advice of General Secundroff,* the
director of public affairs, and went to Būcerdilin,
where he is just now."

OF THE ARMY SENT TO SUCCOUR THE FORTRESS
OF SOKAL.

On the arrival of the above army at Būcerdilin, according to the account of the soldiers, they sent to
Walewe for various necessaries, and afterwards sent
an army to attack Sokal. The illustrious governor
was roused, and determined on remaining no longer
inactive; he ordered a movement to be made, left

* Count Seckendorff.

Asamsha, and pitched his camp at the distance of four hours' journey on the banks of the Drin, directly on the road taken by the enemy. A party of five or six thousand troops (Bosnians), under the command of the often-mentioned Mohammed, were ordered to succour Sokal. One Abaza, a cloth merchant, joined himself to them. An order was also issued for the men of Izernūka and Togla to join themselves to Mohammed's party; and Ali Beg, Agha, and Mustapha Effendi, were appointed leaders to this augmentation. They proceeded in two divisions towards Sokal, in order to attack the enemy: information of the enemy's movement having reached the faithful by means of spies, the chiefs of the Moslem army, with the nobles and officers, met to consult over the matter by the turning of cups, &c.; they hurried on, assured of victory. After three hours' journey they met the enemy, and came within cannon-shot of them. Being thus placed face to face, a desperate struggle commenced. The infidels maintained an obstinate resistance, and so dreadful was the scene, that the very rocks trembled: at length, however, the enemy began to give way, and afterwards took to flight. The victorious Moslems, with the most intrepid courage, pursued them so hard, that they gave them no time to breathe: many of them who escaped the sword, fell into a channel which was on the road they fled by, and perished in it. The pursuing army, in consequence of the night coming on, was obliged to stop at this channel, where they passed the night. Next morning at day-light they proceeded in their pursuit; but the fugitives made towards Walewe, where they were slaughtered in great numbers. Many of the enemy at Būcerdilin also perished. The victorious Moslems returned with immense booty, and above three thousand prisoners.

OF THE TAKING OF THE PALANKA OF WALEWE.

After a few days' rest, the victorious troops proceeded to take this fortress also. They so distressed the infidels in it, that they were compelled to beg for a capitulation. After delivering it over to the victorious army, the infidels who were in it were allowed to make the best of their way to their own army, whilst all the cannon, &c., that were found in it, were transported to the fortress of Sokal, and the Palanka burned down to the ground. The governor in return, ordered splendid presents to be made to all the distinguished persons who accompanied Mohammed, and a robe of honour to be given to the leader himself. Peculiar marks of respect and honour were shewn to Ali Mohammed Agha of Tzwernick, who acted a conspicuous part in the late action with the enemy.

After these things the Moslem camp removed from its position, and in three days reached the borders of Tzwernick with pomp and great glory, and pitched their camp at —— (*the name of the place is left out of the text*).

OF MOHAMMED, AND THE CAPTURE OF THE SOLDIERS
BELONGING TO THE ENEMY.

According to the account given by these soldiers,
the son-in-law of the emperor, though he relinquished
the idea of entering Bosnia and proceeding to Serai,
was still determined to do something. "Let us,"
said he, "not return without some advantage : let
us attack the fortress of Tzwernick, which lies in our
neighbourhood ; it will be easily conquered." Such
were his designs, and after having wickedly determined on putting these designs into execution,
behold he learned from the men who were allowed
to escape from Walewe, the defeat of the army which
he had sent to Sokal, the fate of the palanka of
Walewe ; and that the governor of Bosnia, with his
innumerable army, was encamped before Tzwernick.
This information astonished and confounded the infidels. The governor, in the meantime receiving
information of the state of the enemy, after reaching
Tzwernick, sent the heroic Mohammed with a thousand veterans whom he himself had requested, to
reconnoitre the enemy. Soon after leaving the
camp they fell in with the enemy's picquet, at the
foot of a mountain near a place called Chara, which
they furiously attacked. Those of the enemy who
escaped the sword fled in the utmost confusion :
more than a hundred of them perished ; and Sombal,
the captain of the picquet, and a hundred of these

wretches, were made prisoners, and carried in chains before the most noble governor. The illustrious governor caused the customary honours and rewards to be paid to the conquerors.

Whilst the governor and all his brave Mussulmans were rejoicing over their victories, the son-in-law of the emperor, and the director of affairs, who accompanied him, seeing they were unable to do any thing against Tzwernick, and being unable also to keep possession of Būcerdilin, they without delay threw bridges over the Save, and, like an army of ants, crossed over to their own unhappy dominions.

OF THE RETURN OF THE GOVERNOR AND HIS ARMY TO THE CITY OF SERAI.

The above information being sufficiently confirmed, the governor resolved on remaining a little longer where he was, for the purpose of dispatching affairs : this being accomplished, he determined on returning to Serai, which, by easy and short journies, he accomplished in peace and safety. The various places of the new fortress were soon furnished with their appropriate articles; the magazines were filled with provisions, and the arsenal with all kinds of arms and other stores.

OF BŪCERDILIN.

The wise and sagacious governor, not willing to spend the precious hours in inactivity, ceased not night or day to contemplate how he might distress the enemy, and enrich his victorious warriors with their spoils. After it was demonstrated to him that the enemy had left Būcerdilin, he resolved on sending an army after them into their own country : for this purpose, an order was issued that all the men able to bear arms in the jurisdictions of Tzwernick, Tūzla, and Kladina, should immediately assemble. Agha Ali Beg Mohammed of Tzwernick, Agha Mustapha of Tūzla, and the Capudan of Tzwernick, were appointed to command this army and conduct the enterprise. This expedition set forward in quest of the enemy, and learned from the inhabitants of the palanka called Pernawer, the route they had taken. After receiving this information, they moved hastily forward, and after having intercepted them, killed fifty of them, took fifteen prisoners, and burned their palanka. After performing these deeds of valour, they turned to another palanka called Belina : this they also burned, killed seventy of the enemy, took thirty of them prisoners, and returned to the plains of Tzwernick with immense booty. When the illustrious governor was informed of these splendid exploits, he praised God. In the meantime, it was agreed that his excellency the illustrious governor should make the city of Serai his winter quarters :

not wishing, however, to remain idle during the days
of winter, the illustrious governor invited the effendis, the learned, the lovers of peace, the princes of
the banners, the capudans of the frontiers, and those
experienced in affairs in the various jurisdictions,
to assemble at Serai. When they had all assembled
in the presence of the governor, he said: "You all
know how the treacherous Albanians before our eyes
acted in the case of Ozitcha (which is only twenty-
four hours' journey from this city); how they formed
an alliance with the enemy; how they to their
disgrace and dishonour assisted in burning and destroying several of our palankas; how they shewed
the enemy the roads; and how they persevered in
their treachery and rebellion." After hearing this
speech, and consulting what steps they should take
in order to punish these rebels, it was resolved to
wait the royal mandate about this affair.

OF THE ARMY SENT TO PUNISH THESE REBELLIOUS MOUNTAINEERS.

After the imperial mandate had arrived and its
contents had been considered, it was immediately
resolved, notwithstanding the severity of the winter,
the snow, and the rain, to go and punish the rebel-
lious mountaineers by attacking them in two different quarters at the same time. The place of their
retreat being within deep abysses of difficult access,
the orthodox veterans had hard work to come at

them, having to travel through snow and over preci-
pices. So soon, however, as they found out the
place of these impure wretches, they commenced
the work of destruction. These wretches shewed a
determination to resist, and began firing with great
fury and desperate effect; they killed by their balls
more than a hundred of the nobles and common
people belonging to the fort of Būdghūrisha; but
the orthodox troops slew an immense number of
them. When they perceived that they were unable
to cope with the true believers, and that they had
no mode of escape, they were constrained to sue for
their lives. Before accepting, however, of their
submission, they were required to give hostages as
to their future conduct, which they did. The faithful troops, after having brought this war to a happy
conclusion, returned in triumph to their camp,
carrying with them much booty, besides a number
of prisoners, consisting of women and children. The
chief government conferred on this occasion the
dignity of the principality on Tūrmish Pāshā, Murād
Beg.

After the defeat of the rebels, as above related,
preparations were commenced for retaking Ozitcha.
To accomplish this object fifteen thousand chosen
troops, under the command of Ali Pāshā-Zādah
Ibrahim of ——— (*the name of the place is wanting
in the text*) and the renowned Mohammed, were
ordered for this war. The two commanders were
enjoined to act in concert, and to consult each other
on every measure necessary to be adopted for the

success of the expedition. They were furnished with five pieces of cannon, and other destructive weapons, and ordered to depart. The courageous army, though compelled to make short stages in consequence of the severity of the weather, the rain, and the snow, arrived at length at Ozitcha: they lost no time in preparing to besiege the place, and soon surrounded it.

OF THE ACTIONS OF MOHAMMED IN THIS AFFAIR.

When every thing was in a state of complete preparation, and the place surrounded, the intrepid Mohammed set off with five or six thousand horsemen, Bosnians, and scoured the whole country round, destroyed all the palankas * which environed the fortress, and returned with booty of all kinds to the Moslem camp, from the territories of the enemy.

After a short period of repose spies arrived, who said that the enemy was sending off troops from Belgrade to succour the above place. On this information, the intrepid Mohammed with five or six thousand veterans set out to meet this infidel host, which he did at a place called Rūd. This body of infidel troops, though they shewed some courage, were soon overpowered; some perished, others fled to Belgrade, and some were taken prisoners. The

---

* The context would here imply that the word *palanka* implied a stoccado, as well as a fort. See note, p. 4.

victors returned to the Moslem camp before Ozitcha,
loaded with spoils taken from the enemies of the
Ottoman empire, besides a number of prisoners.

OF THE CONQUEST OF OZITCHA.

When the enemy within this fortress saw no way
of being able to resist effectually the efforts of the
besiegers, and despairing of assistance from any
quarter, they at last capitulated, on the condition of
their lives being spared. After delivering up the
fortress into the hands of the victors, they themselves
were escorted by a body of the faithful as far as
Rūd. When information of this victory was laid
before the august governor, he rejoiced greatly, and
immediately delegated the heroic Mohammed, with
a certain number of troops, to take possession of the
aforesaid fortress, with the view of his arranging
matters within it, and settling affairs in its environs.
Mohammed, after this splendid achievement, had become conspicuous in the eyes of both the noble and
ignoble: the illustrious governor wishing to pro-
mote him, laid his request in his favour at the foot of
the Ottoman throne, when Mahommed, by a royal
mandate, was raised to a principality. At the
same time Ali Pāshā-Zādah Ibrahim had also dignities conferred on him, and on his brother Derwish
Beg, by the government of Romeli.

OF THE CONQUEST OF THE PALANKA OF RŪD
OR RODI.

Whilst the gallant Mohammed was intensely
occupied in the affairs of the fortress to which he
was sent, and making himself acquainted with the
state of the country, he succeeded in bringing all
ranks under proper regulations, in consequence of
the fear he inspired every where. To all the peasants of Chashka, of Rūd, and of Kharaghunisha, who
returned and submitted themselves to him, he gave
every sort of security. But the infidels of Rūd
itself, who had formerly done much mischief at
Yangibazar, about three hundred families, went and
settled at a place called Kharaba, about six hours'
journey from Belgrade. To prevent these infidels,
who might be trusting for aid to the Germans,
injuring the peasants belonging to the Ottoman
empire, and to put these poor people into a state of
security similar to what they enjoyed in former
times, the brave and excellent Mohammed laid their
case before the governor of the kingdom, the illustrious vizir. Measures were immediately adopted
for vanquishing these remaining infidels, and Mohammed was appointed to execute them. The infidels hearing, however, by means of spies, of this
expedition coming against them, they all fled to
Belgrade, leaving every thing behind them. On
Mohammed's coming up to this place, he took

E

possession of all the cannon, &c., which were in it, gathered together all the booty he could find, committed the fortress to some of his men, scoured the country round about, killing the men, and taking the women and children prisoners; left none to offer any further annoyance, and returned with his booty and prisoners in peace and safety to the fortress of Ozitcha, and gave a detailed account of his successes to the illustrious governor.

OF THE BRAVE PEOPLE OF KŪZARISHA.—THE FOLLOWING IS AN ACCOUNT OF ONE OF THE MINOR SKIRMISHES.

There were, in the year last mentioned, in the fortresses of Constanishæ and Dūb, belonging to the enemy, two thousand infernal infidel troops. This execrated troop came by night, with the intention of plundering this city Kūzarisha, and placed themselves in ambush in its vicinity, proposing to themselves to commence their ravages when the followers of Islam met to perform the duties of their religion. It happened, however, when the hour of prayer had arrived, and the public criers had mounted the minarets to announce the same to the people, that one of them by chance saw the lurking-place of the enemy: he immediately descended the minarets, and gave information of what he had discovered. In a moment the news spread, and all the foot and horse within the place rushed suddenly forth and attacked the enemy in their lurking-place, before they succeeded in getting out of it. So very furious was the attack made on them, that they were unable to make any resistance, and fled in confusion ; ninety-six of them perished in the flight, and fifty were taken prisoners : with these last, and about two hundred of their horses, the victors returned in safety to their own place. In this battle only five of the Moslems fell, and seven or eight were wounded. The brother of the commander of the place, Agha Ibrahim, and Mahmūd, a messenger, were dispatched with this intelligence to the illustrious governor. As a confirmation of this news, four of the soldiers who had been taken prisoners were also sent along with them. The venerable governor ordered splendid presents to be made, and great rejoicings were manifested.

OF THE RE-CONQUEST OF THE PALANKA OF DERBEND.

After the enemy was vanquished at Tzwernick, another multitude of infidels attacked the palanka of Derbend, situated near the Save. The garrison and the inhabitants being few in number, were obliged to surrender their place to the enemy, and they themselves took refuge in the surrounding villages. The news of this disaster had scarcely reached Tzwernick, when the scattered Moslems and the inhabitants of the country assembled together, went boldly forward to the fortress, and recovered it out of the hands of the enemy.

OF THE WARRIORS OF NOVI.

In the same year about eighty horse and fifty foot left this place, Novi, with warlike intentions, and attacked a well-peopled village called Glūbofsha, in the neighbourhood of the fortress of Constanishæ, in the enemy's country, and slew all the males with the edge of the sword: the women and children, and all the plunder they could collect, they carried off in triumph. When this event was made known to the people of Ziren, they assembled together and pursued the successful Moslems: two hundred of their number ran forward towards Novi, and took the ford of the river Zerūnishæ, before the orthodox faithful had time to reach it: the remainder, two thousand strong, continued their pursuit, and the orthodox faithful were thus completely hemmed in. When these brave and lion-hearted veterans perceived their condition, they at once drew their swords and fell with fury on the party that obstructed their passage, and soon overcame them: they killed eighty, and made fifty of them prisoners; the rest of them fled in all directions. Those who followed in pursuit no sooner perceived what had happened to their brethren, than their courage also failed them, and they remained in astonishment. The Moslem veterans crossed the

river, and returned to Novi with vast booty besides
those they had taken captives. In this skirmish only
three Moslems fell, and a few were wounded. After
their return they elected one Ahmad, a chief person,
to carry the intelligence of their successes to the
governor. The illustrious governor, besides making
him many presents, raised him to the command of
the artillery, which was confirmed by the Sublime
Porte.

A HEROIC ACHIEVEMENT OF THE MEN OF KŪZARISHA.

The distance between Kūzarisha, on the borders
of the Ottoman empire, and Constanishæ, in the
enemy's country, being only about six hours' journey,
a party of infidels from the environs of the latter
fortress, seventy in number, and thoroughly practised in wickedness, resolved on a plundering excursion into the country of the Moslems; and with this
view came to the neighbourhood of Kūzarisha.

One night, after having indulged themselves in
eating and drinking, they laid themselves carelessly
down to sleep in a hidden part of a wood. A peasant who perceived this came and informed the
commander of Kūzarisha, Omar Capudan, of the
fact, who immediately dispatched a party of eighty
brave veterans, under the command of the celebrated
Ibrahim, called Memku-Oghli, to surprise them.

This party, guided by the peasant who com-

municated the information, soon reached the spot
where the infidels were lying fast asleep, surrounded
them, and quickly overpowered them. In this ren-
counter it is to be lamented that four of the veteran
warriors lost their lives, and five were wounded :
but scarcely one of the enemy escaped being either
killed or taken prisoner. Five principal persons from
among the captives were conducted by the Agha to
the illustrious governor, who, in return, made him
presents of a robe of honour and other valuables.
A present, and instructions respecting the fortress,
were also sent at the same time to the commander
of the fortress, Capudan Omar.

ANOTHER ACHIEVEMENT OF THE MEN OF KŪZARISHA.

On another occasion it happened that a hateful
band of infidels came from the fortress of Gradishka
and attacked two villages, Omashki and Beshtrikah,
in the vicinity of Kūzarisha. Ere they succeeded
however in carrying off the property of the peasants
of these villages, which consisted of household goods,
cattle, and sheep, information from the villagers
reached Kūzarisha. Immediately Capudan Omar,
Memku-Oghli Ibrahim, and Kurd Oghli Omar,
hastened forward to their assistance with a party of
choice warriors, and overtook the infidels at the ford
of Pūzarah, where they attacked them so successfully, as to recover the whole of the booty which

they had so lately taken, besides making several prisoners.

In this skirmish only one of the veterans fell : and information of the whole affair was communicated to the illustrious governor, who made handsome presents to the bearers of the intelligence.

ANOTHER ACHIEVEMENT NEAR NOVI.

The fortress of Constanishæ being only five hours' journey from Novi, and two from the two fortresses on the Ziren, the enemy of religion sought, by various methods, to lay snares for the inhabitants of Novi and its vicinity.

A party therefore, amounting to more than two thousand hateful infidels from these two fortresses, but principally from the suburbs of Constanishæ, consisting of more than a thousand families, divided themselves into three divisions. It was resolved that a division should march on each side of the Una, whilst the third should proceed in boats along that river. This armament was to be directed against Novi, its suburbs, and vicinity.

Having thus settled their diabolical plan of operation, they left Constanishæ by night; and, proceeding towards Novi, the place of their destination, they soon arrived at a place in its neighbourhood called Bolawenshæ; but the brave and intrepid warriors of Novi were by no means ignorant of, or inattentive to, the stratagems employed by the enemy :

they had been informed of the plan of the enemy, and were therefore in a state of complete readiness for receiving them.

The generous and sincere Mohammed Schelevi-Zadah Ahmad Agha, and Fazeli-Zadah Ahmad Agha, ventured, with a body of hardy borderers inured to danger and deeds of valour, and mutually attached, (a favourable omen) to leave Novi the same night, and marched directly to the place where the division of the enemy on this side of the Una had stopped; and, by the assistance of God, completely routed them: two hundred infidels were killed on the spot, and seventy were made prisoners.

The division of the enemy on the opposite side of the river was not much more fortunate. Daz-dār Khalīl Agha, called Murād Sherdil, with another party of associates, attacked them sword in hand, just at the moment when their brethren were engaged on this side in the work of destruction, and dispersed them. Although the enemy's boats were still remaining entire, yet, owing to its being night, none of the divisions of the enemy was able to afford assistance to another: the division in the boats, therefore, proving of no advantage, was soon put to flight, and left a number of dead, whilst others of them fell prisoners into the hands of the conquerors. A great many of their boats were also captured, and the orthodox champions returned triumphantly victorious, and with great joy, to the fortress of Novi.

In this engagement of hostile strife, Mohammed Schelevi-Zadah Ahmad Agha, and Fazeli-Zadah

Ahmad Agha, and a number of their brave followers, fell martyrs for the faith.

The instances now recorded are not the only ones
in which the warriors of Novi were engaged with the
abject infidels. Time would fail to recount the fre-
quent, but similar engagements in which Abubekr
Agha, Zurnik Agha, Husain Agha, and Bekr Agha,
with their respective followers, took a part: they,
by their valour and bravery, spread terror every
where among the infidels of that quarter, even to
their women and children.

AN ACHIEVEMENT OF THE CAPUDAN OF
YANGIBAZAR.

The fortress of Azishæ being in the hands of the
enemy, the Capudan of Yangibazar attacked, with
four or five thousand warriors, the infidels in the
district lying in the neighbourhood of Chashka.
They killed some, took a number of captives, and
returned with the spoils they had taken as far as
Brauvnik, where they halted. In the meantime
Capudan Mattewæshka, the chief commander of
Chashka and Puzghajak and the adjacent country,
pursued the Moslem warriors with a troop amounting to some thousands, and overtook them at the
place where they halted. The Moslem warriors no
sooner perceived this numerous and hostile troop of
infidels coming upon them, than they immediately,
and before allowing them time to commence their

attack, moved to meet the foe, and very soon caused them to retreat with the loss of one hundred and fifty killed, and seventy prisoners : when the orthodox warriors pursued their journey without any further molestation.

AN ACHIEVEMENT OF THE MEN OF OSTERWISHÆ.

It happened that an army of three thousand of Arnaut infidels assembled together, and formed the intention of surprising the inhabitants of Osterwishæ, situate on the extreme borders of Bosnia.

In order to accomplish their machinations, they approached this fortress by night, and carefully circumambulated it in search of the gate, which they found. In consequence of the darkness of the night, and the want of vigilance on the part of the sentinels, they succeeded so far as to place the ladders they had brought along with them to the walls of the fortress without being observed. Their object was to get the gate opened and then to rush in a body into the place. A number of them climbed over the wall, and were just on the eve of getting the gate opened, when, fortunately, in this moment of imminent danger, a woman, who was giving suck to her child, perceived what was going on, and prevented the ruin and subjugation of the garrison. She ran immediately and informed the commander, who instantly caused a musket to be fired off in order to alarm the inhabitants. This succeeded ; and the consequence was, that most of those infidels who had got within the place were seized and killed on the spot. The garrison and the inhabitants, furnished with swords, spears, and javelins, all rushed forth to take vengeance on their daring assailants, and utterly destroyed the greater number of them, and took several prisoners ; the best looking of whom they sent to his excellency the governor.

ANOTHER ACHIEVEMENT.

On a certain occasion eighty of the hardy warriors of Novi entered into a compact to make a hostile excursion. On the night appointed for making this excursion they crossed the Una, and surprised the inhabitants of Kurkoyshuka, about two hours' journey from Novi. Many of the infidels of this place they killed, and returned with much booty and several prisoners. Bachtyār Agha and Karah Mime-Zadah Husain Agha fell in this excursion.

CONCERNING THE ARRIVAL OF THE SUBLIME FIRMAN.

About this time, 1152, (1739,) when the royal mandates were issued, a high firman respecting the ravaging and vexing of the enemy's dominions reached the illustrious governor, from the supreme vizir in the royal camp. In conformity to this firman from the supreme vizir, the governor, skilful in affairs, invited the heads of the principalities, the august emirs, the supreme judges, the experienced men of the borders, and other grandees and great men of the kingdom, capable of giving good counsel and advice, to meet at Medina Serai, for the purpose of consultation on the subject of communication.

It appeared to this council, constituted by the illustrious governor, that, as the countries belonging to the enemy, lying about Constanishæ, on the Ziren, the Una, and the Kopa, had not been thoroughly subdued, properly peopled and cultivated, from the year 1090, (about 1679,)* and as the inhabitants of these districts were exceedingly hostile to the Moslems, they, country and people, should be subjected forthwith to the devastations of war. This was unanimously agreed to. The orthodox army under the command of the governor was ordered to quit Serai, and march towards Novi, on the borders of Bosnia, a distance of forty-eight hours' journey.

By means of bridges they crossed the Una and laid siege to the fortress of Ziren, a short distance

---

* It was about this period that Cara Mustapha, brother-in-law to the celebrated grand vizir Ahmad Kiuperle, whom the Turks eulogise as " the light and splendour of nations, the conserver and guardian of good laws, the vicar of the shadow of God, the thrice-learned and accomplished !" led a prodigious army of Osmanlies across the Danube, let loose forty thousand Tartars who ravaged and desolated the frontiers of Austria, Bohemia, and Moravia, and who, in 1683, presented himself before the walls of Vienna with one hundred and eighty thousand men, and nearly succeeded in reducing that city.

from Novi. This sudden and unexpected movement of the orthodox troops inspired the abject infidels every where around with terror and consternation, and caused them to seek an asylum somewhere else, whilst their contemptible leaders took to their heels; thus leaving the vacant fortress to the invading army, who placed a garrison in it.

OF THE DEVASTATION OF THE ENEMY'S COUNTRY.

After the event above related, troop after troop was successively appointed and sent forth to ravage and destroy the enemy's country. Their movements might be compared to mighty streams which inundate the earth: they overwhelmed every district belonging to the idolatrous enemy* as far as Constanishæ, the Nū, the Dūl, and other rivers, even to the Kopa; fought and gained many battles; and returned successively and successfully with immense spoils of war to the Moslem camp.

The fortress of Ziren before mentioned, it ought to be observed, was plied and battered with cannon-shot and shells. The buildings, both inside and outside the fortress, were all either burned or destroyed; the fortifications and walls were all thrown down: it was, notwithstanding, taken with difficulty.

Though Ziren is not far from Constanishæ, and

---

* The Mohammedans always term the Christians idolaters because of their belief in the Trinity. The word translated *idolaters* is *mushrakin;* literally, *those who give partners (to God).*

even within the possibility of obtaining aid from it, and also from Ghuzdansak, yet neither of these two fortresses found it practicable to give it any.

After the fall of Ziren, and the performance of other exploits, the impetuous and high-spirited borderers returned to Novi where they remained for some days, and then directed their march towards the free provinces, and encamped at a place called Tūmenah.

OF THE ARRIVAL OF THE TARTAR ARMY.

Whilst the camp of the Moslems remained at the above place, and after the Tatar (Tartar) troops come from the east, according to ancient law and custom, had joined it, the chief leaders of the army of Islamites, the men of the borders, and others eminent for counsel, formed themselves into a council of war. After conferring together in cheering and reviving concord, and in dialogue of circulating cups, it was finally and unanimously agreed that a body of troops, amounting to six thousand, should be chosen from among the men of the borders, and from among the heroes of Bosnia, and placed under the command of the governor's deputy, Yākūb Agha. The Tartar troops were attached to this army: and the whole presented an aspect that predicted victorious and glorious results.

Kinzawæ, Dūbishæ, and Yasnoffshæ, with their various dependencies on the east side of the Una,

were fixed on as the field whereon this appointed
army was destined to carry on its work of devastation. Like an impetuous flood, therefore, it entered
into these countries or districts, and carried fire and
sword to the very verge of that river, swept away
every thing that opposed its progress, took vast
quantities of spoil, such as sheep and large cattle,
household goods, and chattels, besides slaves; and
thus fully and effectually chastised the enemies of
the Moslems.

A BATTLE WITH THE ENEMY.

It so happened, in the meantime, that the enemy
concentrated some forces before the fortress of Isla-
bin, with the intention of doing violence and damage
to the Ottoman dominions.

However, the united and harmonious army of the
Islamites came unexpectedly upon them, and attacked them with lion-like fury. The contest was
hot and doubtful for a while ; but the arrival of the
Tartar troops soon decided the fate of the enemy.
These, in furious rage, attacked them with their
arrows, spears, and swords ; and the enemy being
unable to maintain their ground any longer, took to
their heels, leaving many killed and wounded.

The remnant of the enemy fled to the other side
of Una, where they afterwards sold their lives as
dear as possible. Being greatly exasperated, and
having in some degree recovered their courage, they

imagined they had now obtained a more favourable position, and began to make a pompous show of their remaining strength.

The Moslem warriors, in the meantime, carefully explored the banks of the river; and on a night previously fixed on, the men of the borders and the Tartars crossed over, and immediately attacked their position. The enemy perceiving however that they were unable to resist the superior force which the Moslems brought against them, their apparent firmness gave way; and in a short time their whole camp was in full flight towards the Save, but hotly pursued by the conquering Moslems, who did not give up their pursuit till they were stopped by that river.

Great numbers of these idolatrous infidels were totally annihilated, and a great number more fell into the hands of their pursuers. The Islamite troops, in order to take full vengeance on the enemy on account of their aggressions, plundered the country, burned and destroyed the towns and villages situate on the banks of the Una, killed the men, carried off all the women and children, and returned with their spoils to the Islamite camp.

THE GOVERNOR'S DEPARTURE FOR TRAUNICK.

Praise be to God! The countries belonging to the enemy having been thus chastised and spoiled, the august commands of the Ottoman emperor were fully accomplished : it was therefore judged proper to return to Traunick, the seat of government and jurisdiction ; where the winter was spent in making fresh preparations for commencing operations again in the spring of the year.

A FIRMAN ARRIVES REQUIRING THE GOVERNOR TO MARCH TO BELGRADE.

Whilst engaged in making preparations, as before hinted, for commencing the operations of war anew, in consulting about measures proper to be adopted, in conversing, and in considering and examining affairs, the happy days of spring arrived, which announced that the moment for active operations was now come.

At this time the royal firman, obeyed by all the world, reached the illustrious governor, requiring him to unite himself and his Bosnian troops, with those in the royal camp under the command of his excellency the grand vizir.

His excellency the dignified governor having arranged matters for the better security of the Ottoman frontiers, placed garrisons every where; and having attended to other affairs of government of high importance, he and his army quitted Traunick and pitched his camp in the plains of ——, to which the other Moslem troops were required to repair.

Experienced warriors from Serai, Tzwernick, and other places ; princes, distinguished aghas, the reverend judge of Serai, the chief judges, and capudans, joined the governor's camp, which soon afterwards commenced moving towards Belgrade, now become the seat of war.

They passed by Tzwernick, crossed at Būcerdilin, and joined the royal camp, actively engaged under the command of his excellency the grand vizir in the siege of Belgrade.

By the instrumentality of one Abdallah Schelevi, a man skilled in arts and sciences, which he had sucked in with his mother's milk, and one of the thousand artificers of Medina Serai,—by the instrumentality of this man, artificial portable bridges had been constructed, and were usually, as occasion required, carried in waggons. By means of these bridges, easily and quickly placed, the army crossed without difficulty the rivers and ravines it had to pass on its way to Belgrade.

OF THE OPERATIONS OF ANOTHER ARMY AGAINST THE DOMINIONS OF THE ENEMY.

This army, consisting of warriors from Traunick, Ak-Hisar, Yaishæ, Banialuka, Kūzarisha, Novi, Behka, Osterwīshæ, Osterwitch-atyk, and other places, had for its leaders Ali Pāshā-Zādah, Ibrahim Pāshā, and Salih Pāshā-Zādah, Mahmūd Pāshā, who were all chosen from the heads of the principalities.

This army, destined to carry war into the interior

of the enemy's country, assembled in the plains of Bilan. Its chiefs and other officers, after much deliberation as to how and where they might more effectually commence hostilities against the enemy, at length agreed, that as the Kūtar country had not for a considerable time past felt the weight of the Moslem arm, it should now feel it. The inhabitants of this district had become proud and haughty, and their mischievous dispositions were to be no longer tolerated.

This army accordingly quitted Bilan, and shortly afterwards overran the whole of the devoted territories of Lyka,* Odwina, Waretshæ and Kūtar, as far as Tawartshæ. The Kūtar country was visited with all the devastations of war. With the vile and despicable idolatrous infidels of these quarters many a hot battle was fought, in which the enemy was always vanquished : yet many of the brave and heroic Islamites drank the sweet sherbet of martyrdom, and many more were wounded; whilst immense numbers of the disgusting and execrated infidels perished, and went to perdition. The victorious warriors returned with great glory to their respective countries laden with rich spoil.

When tidings of this joyful affair was carried to the distinguished army of Islamites in the royal camp employed against Belgrade, the whole host of Mussulmans rejoiced with great exultation. The

* Lyka being again mentioned here, confirms the conjecture already thrown out, that it relates to Hungary. See Note, p. 4.

grand vizir and his excellency the governor presented the bearers of the intelligence with robes of
honour.

THE GOVERNOR'S MANNER WITH THE INHABITANTS.

His excellency the venerable and illustrious governor secured to himself, by his knowledge of war,
his superior skill and consummate prudence, the
love and esteem of all the inhabitants of the kingdom, but especially of those on the frontiers of
Bosnia. Mohammed Pasha, son of Mohammed Beg,
belonging to an ancient family in Bosnia, a feudal
chief, secured to himself much honour and respect,
in consequence of the disinterested zeal he manifested in all the affairs of the country, and never
withdrew himself, during the government of the
governor, for a moment from that interest. Mohammed Pasha was not forgotten in the distribution
of favours: the prime minister raised him, as he
did the renowned Capudan Mohammed, to the
principality of Semendria for his services. The
Capudan Mohammed was raised to the government
of Tzwernick.

As the governor's removal was to take place in
six months, he thought proper to get Mohammed
Beg, Capudan of Yaitsha, raised to be governor of
Banialuka, in consequence of the bravery which he
manifested at Osterwitch-atyk and elsewhere.

At the conclusion of this fortunate war, a party

of five hundred Janissaries and a number of aghas were sent to garrison Tzwernick. Those of them who, from the commencement of the war to its close, had continued to aid the governor in his operations of war, and who had been in the battles and sieges which had taken place, were all ordered to be rewarded as follows, and according to an ancient custom of the country ; viz. to each Agha forty, to each standard-bearer twenty, and to each common man seven pieces of money as wages per day.

So when it pleased God to grant the favour of vanquishing Belgrade, and of forcing the enemy to make peace,* permission was given to the army of Bosnia to return to Serai ; which the governor and the army did.

CONCLUSION, DESCRIPTIVE OF THE COUNTRY AND
INHABITANTS OF BOSNIA.

The kingdom of Bosnia forms a division of the Ottoman empire, and is a key to the countries of Roumeli (or Romeli). Although its length and breadth be of unequal dimensions, yet it is not improper to say it is equal in climate to Misr and Sham (Egypt and Syria). Each one of its lofty mountains, exalted to Ayuk, (a bright red star that

---

* The peace of Belgrade was signed on the first of September, 1739. By this peace the treaty of Passarowitz was nullified, and the rivers Danube, Save, and Una re-established, as the boundaries of the two empires. See note to page 1.

always follows the Hyades,) is an eye-sore to a foe.

By reason of this country's vicinity to the infidel nations, such as the deceitful Germans, Hungarians, Serbs (Sclavonians), the tribes of Croats, and the Venetians, strong and powerful, and furnished with abundance of cannon, muskets, and other weapons of destruction, it has had to carry on fierce war from time to time with one or other, or more, of these deceitful enemies—enemies accustomed to mischief, inured to deeds of violence, resembling wild mountaineers in asperity, and inflamed with the rage of seeking opportunities of putting their machinations into practice; but the inhabitants of Bosnia know this. The greater part of her peasants are strong, courageous, ardent, lion-hearted, professionally fond of war, and revengeful: if the enemy but only show himself in any quarter, they, never seeking any pretext for declining, hasten to the aid of each other. Though in general they are harmless, yet in conflict with an enemy they are particularly vehement and obstinate; in battle they are strong-hearted; to high commands they are obedient, and submissive as sheep; they are free from injustice and wickedness; they commit no villany, and are never guilty of high-way robbery; and they are ready to sacrifice their lives in behalf of their religion and the emperor. This is an honour which the people of Bosnia have received as an inheritance from their forefathers, and which every parent bequeaths to his son at his death.

By far the greater number of the inhabitants, but especially the warlike chiefs, capudans, and veterans of the borders, in order to mount and dismount without inconvenience, and to walk with greater freedom and agility, wear short and closely fitted garments : they wear the fur of the wolf and leopard about their shoulders, and eagles' wings in their caps, which are made of wolf-skins. The ornaments of their horses are wolf and bear-skins : their weapons of defence are the sword, the javelin, the axe, the spear, pistols, and muskets : their cavalry are swift, and their foot nimble and quick. Thus dressed and accoutred they present a formidable appearance, and never fail to inspire their enemies with a dread of their valour and heroism.

So much for the events which have taken place within so short a space of time.* It is not in our power to write and describe every thing connected with the war, or which came to pass during that eventful period. Let this suffice.

---

* It will be seen by the dates given in page 1, that the war lasted about two years and five months.

Prepared and printed from the rare and valuable collection of Omer Effendi of Novi, a native of Bosnia, by Ibrahim.*

* This Ibrahim was called Basmajee, the printer. He is mentioned in history as a renegado, and to have been associated with the son of Mehemet Effendi, the negotiator of the peace of Passarowitz, and who was, in 1721, deputed on a special embassy to Louis XV. Seyd Effendi, who introduced the art of printing into Turkey. Ibrahim, under the auspices of the government, and by the munificence of Seyd Effendi aiding his labours, succeeded in sending from the newly instituted presses several works, besides the Account of the War in Bosnia.

www.ingramcontent.com/pod-product-compliance
Ingram Content Group UK Ltd.
Pitfield, Milton Keynes, MK11 3LW, UK
UKHW042150280225
455719UK00001B/253